Reviews

Gillian Morris has certainly met her goal of inviting people to be open to exploring tapping by pulling together interesting stories and examples from a broad assortment of practitioners on various ways EFT / tapping can be applied. Tapping could help the readers live fuller lives, decrease their pain and suffering, and release the traumas that haunt them.

Mary Ayers, PhD

The power of EFT / tapping in the world is growing, as evidenced by this collection of different authors who are changing people's lives with the technique. In addition to having the technique taught step-by-step, reading the different stories, and hearing about the benefits of EFT in such a conversational way is great. Kudos, Gillian, for the contribution to improving the lives of people everywhere.

Pamela Bruner

Business Coach, co-author of: Tapping into Ultimate Success

People who know me through my own work as one of only 28 EFT Masters worldwide know that my passion is to share EFT with all who want to help themselves, and those close to them, to live happier, healthier and more fulfilling lives.

It is clear that Gillian and her fellow contributors share my passion for this amazing self-help and therapeutic tool that provides astounding results time and again and I applaud their efforts to take EFT to a larger audience.

Gary Craig, the creator of EFT says we should 'try it on everything' and this book goes a long way to highlighting the number of diverse areas in which it can work. As the title suggests, there is something here for *Everyone.*

Karl Dawson

EFT Founding Master and creator of Matrix Reimprinting

Author of: Matrix Reimprinting Using EFT: Rewrite Your Past, Transform Your Future and Transform Your Beliefs, Transform Your Life, EFT Tapping using Matrix Reimprinting.

This book is a summary of what EFT is and how some experienced practitioners use EFT in their practice. It was easy to read and I found it fascinating how many applications there are for EFT. I learnt basic EFT some years ago and used it for younger patients with needle phobias. Now, I realise that EFT is not just for phobias or for emergencies and I am inspired to tap every day for everything!

Recently, I suffered from breast cancer and during my treatment, I read how important it is to clear negative emotions from the body in order to maintain health and to prevent recurrence. I just did not know how to do it. Talking about feelings, writing them down and having counselling helped but the emotions were still there. I wanted a way of physically clearing the negative emotions from my body. It turns out EFT is the method I was looking for. I just had not yet realised it.

EFT is great for maintaining autonomy and as part of taking responsibility for one's own health.

I am currently training as a shamanic practitioner. It was interesting to read how EFT can be combined with many other healing modalities, both conventional and alternative, in a complementary way to enhance practice. I look forward to doing this myself in the future.
Dr Mary Hernon
Former consultant obstetrician and gynaecologist

I have to say that EFT for Everyone reads really well. It is very interesting to see just how EFT can help in lots of different situations in everyday life. It is nice to learn how the authors of each chapter found EFT and how it has helped them and their clients move forward in their lives in a more positive and successful way.

I think it should be a very successful book as it explains EFT in a simplistic way, including the many different areas of life one may come across, the inclusion of client feedback is really helpful and enlightening too.

Thank you for giving me the opportunity to do this review. I look forward to using EFT both personally and professionally in the future. I think lots of people will enjoy the book as there is indeed something in it for *Everyone.*
Helen Humphries
Equine manager

EFT for Everyone is a great book for both the sceptic and the open-minded. Traditional medicine is failing big time because it treats the body as small individual parts, the holistic approach in my opinion is the best way to support your body in being as healthy as possible including dealing with ailments.

Our emotions also play a role in having an effect on our health. This book tells the stories of many people facing all kinds of problems. EFT in combination with regular exercise and healthy nutrition offers a truly holistic approach to getting you back into balance. I found it a very informative read and also useful as a reference book, with so many different cases discussed. Highly recommended for all those looking at truly doing their best in life!

Fabrizio Poli

Author of: Your Attitude Determines Your Altitude, Born to Fly and Health4Flyers

EFT for Everyone

Life Changing Techniques At Your Fingertips

Gillian E. Morris

Disclaimer

The information given in this book is intended for informational purposes only and should not be used or construed to be a substitute for professional advice or medical care. Any use of the information in this book is at the reader's own risk and discretion. The authors and publishers cannot be held responsible for any loss, claim, or damage arising out of any suggestions made, or the use or misuse of any material on third party websites.

ISBN-13: 9781907415029
ISBN-10: 1907415025

Zento Publishing
8 Glendene Avenue
Bramhall
Cheshire
SK7 1BH

Contents Page

Foreword

In my forty-year career as a transformational speaker, trainer and coach, I have encountered hundreds of thousands of people who want to change their lives for the better. Despite their initial enthusiasm, however, many of them have trouble getting started or sustaining their efforts because of negative thoughts and limiting beliefs that hold them back.

I have found that EFT is an easy to learn yet extremely powerful technique for removing those barriers that are stopping you from getting from where you are to where you want to be. I use it in almost all of my workshops and coaching sessions, and have seen the amazing results it produces over and over.

I am excited that you are reading this book, and I recommend that you read it in its entirety as soon as possible because, whatever is going on in your life, as soon as you begin applying these techniques, you are going to see a dramatic change for the better.

As the title implies, EFT is a technique that can benefit *everyone* in every area of your life—health, wealth, happiness, relationships, parenting, athletic performance, and work. It can be used to heal past traumas, remove limiting beliefs, dissolve fear, guilt and other negative emotions, and overcome internal blocks to personal and professional success.

In addition to releasing the negative impact of past events, EFT can also be used as a daily discipline. If you are smart, EFT will become a daily habit to release any negative thoughts and emotions and other stressors that arise during the day, just as you brush your teeth every day.

In the first half of *EFT for Everyone* Gillian brilliantly presents the marvellous versatility of EFT and the many diverse areas in which you can easily apply it. She also gives you a clear primer on the fundamentals of the basic technique of EFT. In the following chapters, her co-authors share their personal experiences with using EFT in their own life and with their coaching and counselling clients. These chapters will deepen and expand your understanding of the life-changing power of this gentle, simple to learn, yet incredibly powerful technique.

I strongly encourage you to use this valuable book to its full advantage and enjoy the amazing benefits of EFT for yourself, your family, and the people you work with. I promise you that you will be forever grateful that you did.

—Jack Canfield, co-author of *The Success Principles*™ and creator of the #1 New York Times best-selling *Chicken Soup for the Soul*® series.

Introduction

Never in a million years would I have thought that an ordinary person like me, just a 'regular lass from Lancashire', could have written and published a book. The fact that you are reading this book is a testament to the topic itself: Emotional Freedom Techniques (EFT), also known as 'Tapping', and how it could change your life, as it did mine.

I was first introduced to EFT, in 2009, by a close friend from work. I was in a dark place back then: struggling with emotional and physical issues, generally just not coping. Everything was such a struggle. Normal everyday tasks seemed insurmountable and although I did keep going, I have to admit, it was incredibly hard.

Eventually, I went to the doctors and got some medication, which helped me to cope, in a manner of speaking. I stopped feeling so low. In fact, I stopped feeling pretty much altogether. I was just numb. I was very blessed with a good support network of family and friends and my faith also played a big part in helping me through that difficult time. Looking back now, I do not really remember much about it, maybe that is a good thing.

I tried tapping, by looking it up on a website, and it did seem a bit weird at first. However, because I had qualified as a reflexologist previously,

I understood the principles of the meridians in the body and believed in energy therapy.

I found that it did help a bit, but because of my condition and the medication I was taking, I did not benefit from it as much as I now know I could have done if I had persisted, or, better still, worked with a qualified practitioner.

I participated in the online Tapping World Summits of 2012 and 2013. After the 2013 summit, I felt so great that I decided I had to go and learn EFT and become a practitioner myself. I did some research and found that one of the twenty-nine EFT Founding Masters; Tania A. Prince ran courses in Manchester, not too far from my home. I booked the course straight away, and the rest, as they say, is history. At that time, my back was very painful and I knew I could not drive to Manchester and back for 3 consecutive days so I booked a hotel too. This was quite out of character for me but I knew how much I wanted to do it.

I loved the training! Tania was fabulous and I felt relaxed with her personally and with her style of teaching. After the 3 days I felt like I was 'walking on air'. The follow-up training, case studies, supervision, research and then going on to work with clients have been a fantastic learning journey for me.

I no longer take the maximum daily allowance of painkillers. In fact, I very rarely take any painkillers at all, which is a great blessing and much better for my body. I am much more active and able to do more things, I visit different places and I enjoy myself more – I feel very blessed. It has been a real transformation. Slowly but surely, I began to improve in every aspect of my life: physically, emotionally, energetically, my focus: yep, everything. People began to comment on how much I was changing, how I seemed better and happier. I felt like the 'real me' was emerging. My confidence improved almost in line with the growth of my skills.

I have to be honest and say that I was hooked! I loved EFT and everything about it. The more I researched it, the more I wanted to know and the more I wanted to tell everyone!

The case studies I did at the beginning were amazing to me. Furthermore, as I have progressed and worked with an increasing number of people, the results have not changed and they still continue to amaze me. I have met some wonderful people and have enjoyed helping others learn EFT and use it in their lives too.

I am very blessed to be involved in this work and to have met such fantastic, kind, helpful people. That is what inspired me to write this book. To share EFT with as many people as possible and to give back at least some of the blessings I have received.

The wonderful co-authors of the book have shared their introduction to EFT and how they have used it to help themselves and others. I wanted to include a wide variety of examples and thought that this was the perfect way to achieve it. They are an inspiration to me and I hope they are for you too.

The more I continue to research and work with EFT, the more I am convinced that it is a tool which can be useful for everybody in the whole world. I want to reach as many people as I can. I think it is life changing and if we can change lives for the better, then surely we can change the world for the better.

EFT: What is it?

Emotional Freedom Techniques – EFT / Tapping, works with the body's energy systems.

It is a form of energy therapy. Some well-known energy therapies you may have already heard of are acupuncture, acupressure, reflexology and reiki.

EFT is a blend of modern-day psychology and ancient Chinese acupressure. It uses the meridians of the body (from acupressure) to help the body's energy flow naturally and freely.

Gary Craig, the developer of EFT, states: 'The cause of all negative emotions is a disruption in the body's energy system.'

This means that any emotional upset or trauma can disrupt the body's energy system and be stored in our bodies as negative emotions or feelings. Unless we unblock them, they will stay stuck in our memory and affect our health and well-being.

Tapping on the meridian points sends kinetic energy down the energy system, clearing the blockages and allowing the energy to flow freely again. Once we have released this emotional charge we will no longer feel negative emotions when we think about the negative experiences. We can still recall the memories but without the negative emotions that go with them. It can also give us relief from physical symptoms and, once we have cleared these, it allows us to move forward with our lives with more clarity, freedom and peace.

EFT uses fingertips instead of needles to tap on the acupressure points. It is a non-invasive self-help technique; easy to learn and to use. Professionals helping war veterans and severely traumatized people have used EFT with great success.

EFT: How to do it

The purpose of this book is to get EFT out to as many people as possible. It is not a textbook on how to do EFT, therefore I will only be explaining the EFT Basic Tapping Recipe (sequence) which is straightforward and generally only takes a few minutes to learn. With a little practice, you will perform each round in approximately one minute. I have listed some further resources and reading at the back of the book, should you wish to learn more about EFT.

I tap using my index finger and middle finger, other people may use one finger or more, it does not really matter. You can use either hand, depending which feels the most comfortable for you. The majority of the tapping points are on both sides of the body and so it does not matter which side you tap on. Some people like to tap on both sides. You can switch sides during the tapping, or alternate the sides. It really is a flexible process in that respect. If you prefer, you can tap on both sides of the body at the same time, some therapists like to do it this way. Most people use their dominant hand as it feels more natural.

Ideally, you will use your fingertips, not your finger pads, however, if you have long fingernails you should of course use your finger pads, otherwise you may end up stabbing yourself! Many meridians start or end at the fingertips so, as you tap, you will be stimulating the energy meridians there. This is why it is better to tap with your fingertips than with an object or another body part but you can use a flat hand on the collar bone, underarm and head if that is more comfortable for you.

When you tap, you use the same amount of pressure as you would if you were strumming gently on a table top. Ideally, you should tap around 5-7 times on each point but the actual number is not critical. While it is important to tap the correct area, you do not need to worry about being absolutely precise, as tapping the general area is sufficient. You may also want to remove any watches, bracelets or glasses for comfort. Some people like to close their eyes. This is entirely down to individual choice but try it and see what you prefer.

The tapping points, and their abbreviations, are explained on the following table plus a chart showing the points on the body for easy recognition and quick referencing. (See Table 1 & Diagram 1)

There are other points which people use for tapping. However, the ones listed here are the ones most common and the ones I use.

Tapping Points Chart

Tapping Points	Abbreviation	Location
Karate Chop/ Side of hand	KC / SH	Side of hand between bottom of little finger and wrist
Eyebrow	EB	Start of the eyebrow at side of the nose
Side of the Eye	SE	On the bone at the corner of the eye
Under the Eye	UE	On the bone under the eye below your pupil
Under the Nose	UN	Below nose / above upper lip
Chin	CH	Middle of chin, on crease line
Collar Bone	CB	Start where the knot of a tie would be, move your fingers down 2" and then out 2".
Under the Arm	UA	Under arm on line with nipple
Top of the Head	TH	In the middle of the highest point on top of head

(Table 1)

Tapping Points Diagram

(Diagram for quick referencing)

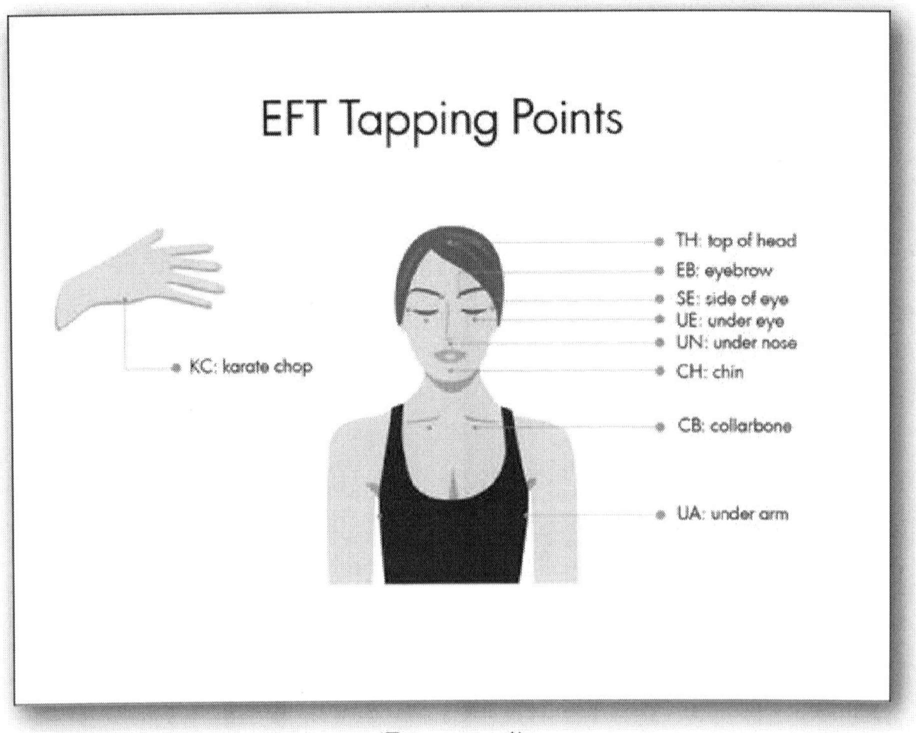

(Diagram 1)

Some examples are:

> "Even though I *have this fear of spiders*, I deeply and completely accept myself anyway."
> "Even though I *feel sick because I have a migraine*, I deeply and completely accept myself anyway."
> "Even though I *am feeling really angry*, I deeply and completely accept myself anyway."
> "Even though I *am upset because my friend has passed away*, I deeply and completely accept myself anyway."

It may seem strange to mention the negative first but this is how we acknowledge our feelings and focus our thinking mind and subconscious on the issue we are working on. We follow this with a positive statement to allow you to accept who you are and that you are working on this issue.

5. *Go through the tapping sequence*

You now tap on each of the points shown in the chart and diagram whilst saying a phrase or word at each point that is linked to the 'Set up' statement e.g. "I feel sick," "I have a migraine," "I am feeling really angry." You can also use the intensity and position during the sequence e.g. "It is the intensity of a 9," "It feels like a knot in my stomach." Use any words that you relate to the issue. Tap through the points, you can go through the points more than once if you feel you need to. Now take a deep breath, in through the nose and out through the mouth, making a sound on the out breath as though you are slowly blowing out a candle.

6. *Reassess the intensity and repeat the process as necessary*

When you have completed the sequence, you reassess the intensity and position of the feeling in your body and go through the process until you get the intensity down to a 2 or below, preferably down to 0. If you have already got to a 2 or 0 then you can just take a few minutes taking deep, calming breaths and enjoying the relief that you have achieved.

Here is an example scenario:

1 Decide the issue you would like to work on
"I am worried about an exam"
2 Rate the intensity on a scale of 0-10 (SUDS)
"Intensity is 8"
3 Locate the position that you feel it in your body
"I feel it in my stomach"
4 Say the 'Set up Statement' (3 times)
Tap on the Karate chop point and say, "Even though I am worried about my exam, I totally and completely accept myself anyway."
5 Go through the tapping sequence
Eye brow: *"I am worried about my exam"*
Side of eye: *"all this worry about my exam"*

Under eye: *"I feel it in my stomach"*
Under nose: *"the intensity is 8"*
Chin point: *"this exam worry"*
Collar bone: *"this worry in my stomach"*
Under arm: *"all this worry"*
Top of head: *"this exam worry"*
Take a deep breath and then let the breath out slowly.

6 Reassess the issue; intensity (SUDS), position and repeat as necessary using the updated information
The intensity is now a 5 and the position in my body is the same.
Repeat the process until you get the SUDS to 2 or below.

It really is that simple! It really is for EVERYONE!

Children love to do it, you can make it fun and tap along to nursery rhymes, favourite songs or even just spelling their name. I have worked with elderly people who like it so much that they do it daily to help stay calm and ease their worries, aches and pains. They have used it to stay calm and cope better during difficult situations e.g. hospital appointments and funerals.

Why not give it try?

EFT: For yourself

Gary Craig, the developer of EFT, encourages us to tap on ourselves every day, not only when stressed or working on a current issue. I like the saying; 'prevention is better than cure.'

I always say to my clients that if you wanted to get a fit, healthy body, you would give it good, nutritious food every day, plenty of water and some form of exercise. Why is it then that most people only do complementary/self-help techniques as a last resort?

If you use tapping when you are stressed, it will definitely help you feel calmer and more relaxed. I will try to show this by using the SUD Scale of 0 to 10. (see Table 2)

The more often you tap, the more you are sending messages to your subconscious that you want to feel calm and relaxed. Things do not bother/trigger you in the same way and some issues that you had will be released without you even noticing.

Gary Craig encourages us, when we have been using tapping for a while and feel calmer and more able to cope, to use a procedure he calls the 'Personal Peace Procedure'.

SUD Scale	
10	10 is the highest intensity of stress you can feel. Tapping at this point will definitely help lower your stress levels.
9	
8	
7	
6	
5	5 is the halfway mark. You are able to cope with the stress but it is still not great to have. At this point, you can still lower your stress levels but may find an underlying issue, or 'trigger', which sends you back up maybe to 8.
4	
3	
2	
1	Continue to tap daily even if you are only on 1 or 0 and do not feel stressed at all. If you do hit a 'trigger' then you may only go up to 5, which is a brilliant improvement!
0	

(Table 2)

This is where you make a list of things from your past, which, when you think about them, still bring up negative emotions of an intensity of 5 or more. You then work through the list, tapping out the negative feelings until you can think of the memory without any negative emotions. **N.B.** it is important to state here that if you have major issues regarding any type of abuse or severe trauma then it is strongly advised that you work with a qualified practitioner who will guide you on how to clear them. Do not try it on your own. I call these 'big T' traumas as opposed to 'little T' traumas, (not to trivialize little traumas as they can make a real impact on people's lives too, but to differentiate between the two).

It is important that, when using EFT or any complementary therapy, that you take full responsibility for your own health and wellbeing. They are not meant to replace medical or psychological treatments you may be having. It would be best if you could use it in conjunction with your medical practitioner.

I have been pleasantly surprised to realise that some issues I had, have just gone, due to me tapping on other issues. It can be strange at first but the more you do it, the more natural it becomes – still amazing, but natural.

EFT: Or bust!

I don't mean broke and I don't mean to the exclusion of everything else, so what do I mean by that?

I have been brought up using various sayings that have been passed on to me by my family, or I have picked up in society or from the media. Unfortunately, or fortunately as the case may be, I use a lot of phrases from TV, films and songs in my everyday life.

A few you might know are:

'I'll be back.' (*Terminator*)

'What you talkin' about, Willis?' (*Different Strokes*)

'Should have gone to Specsavers.' (*TV advert*)

'If you don't have anything good to say, don't say nothing at all.' (*Bambi*)

'If I only had a brain.' (*The Wizard of Oz*)

You get the gist.

'EFT or bust' means to me that I will use it for everything, which I do. Sometimes, slightly later than I should have, but I do tap everyday on something.

Whilst discussing the versatility and application of EFT with my clients, colleagues and friends, I find that quite a lot only tap when they are stressed about something or as a last resort.

My advice is to tap even when you do not think you are feeling stressed. It can still send messages to help your subconscious brain calm down.

Some people, who have been using EFT for a long time, have gone on to develop their own style of EFT. You will find quite a few varieties on the internet. Here is a list of just a few:

EFT & Matrix Reimprinting	Karl Dawson
SET: Simple Energy Techniques	Steve Wells/David Lake
TBT: Trauma Busting Technique	Rehana Webster
Positive EFT	Silvia Hartmann
Matrix Birth Reimprinting	Sharon King

Karl Dawson goes into the memory of the issue and uses what is called an **E**nergetic **C**onsciousness **H**ol**O**gram **E.C.H.O.** for short. Pete Weaver mentions this in more detail in his chapter on sports.

Even though these people and others may use some different tapping points or phrases, they have had success with their style of EFT. Who am I to say what is right for you or anybody else? The main thing, in my opinion, is that they are using the tapping points to release negative energies and emotions so that people can live happier, healthier lives.

As already mentioned, I was trained by Tania A. Prince using Classic EFT, which is what I use in my practice. Sometimes, I will pair it with some visualization or breathing exercises to help the client relax so that they benefit more from the whole experience.

I know that you rarely get a 'one size fits all' and, in all honesty, a few of my clients have not had the same amazing results as other clients. My take on this is the same as Gary Craig's: 'Be specific and be consistent.' If you do not get the results you want straight away, keep at it. Work with a practitioner who can help you find the technique that works best for you, and most of all, keep doing it yourself in-between sessions.

There are sceptics out there, (as there are for most things if you look for them). Some are very aggressive, with strong opinions. Again I would say to them, do not knock it until you have tried it and if it is not for you then please do not put other people off, as they may benefit from it.

I have found that, the more my clients use it, the more success they have. A couple of clients have not achieved the goal that they originally set out to achieve but they admit that they have found some relief in using EFT and may have not been consistent enough in their use of the technique.

Lives of countless people have been changed around the world with EFT...

After the dreadful shooting at an Elementary School in Sandy Hook, Newtown, Connecticut, the Tapping Solution Foundation was formed by Nick, Jessica and Alex Ortner. They have been doing amazing work with the children, parents, teachers, first responders and members of the local community.

http://www.tappingsolutionfoundation.org/the-tapping-solution-for-newtown/

They brought in Dr. Lori Leyden who headed the foundation from December 2012 to December 2015. It was the first US community based trauma healing project using EFT.

Lori has experience of working with trauma survivors and heads the work with genocide victims in Rwanda. She is now pursuing her own work called Project Light and Create Global Healing full time.

http://tappingsolutionfoundation.org/ProjectLight>

https://www.createglobalhealing.org/

EFT Founding Master Tania A. Prince supported 'Empowering the Philippines' – a humanitarian project in which EFT practitioners went to the Philippines to use EFT to relieve suffering after the typhoon in 2013.

http://www.theeftcentre.com/

These are examples of how EFT has been used to ease trauma and suffering and has helped to change lives. I know my life has changed by using it and it has changed the lives of many of my clients, as you can see in my next chapter.

EFT: With clients

Here are a few experiences my clients have kindly shared about EFT.

Spider Phobia

My very first session was with a friend who I knew had a serious spider phobia. I have to admit; I was nervous but very excited to put EFT into practice. I explained what we were going to do and went through the protocol I had been shown to use for phobias. We could not test if it had worked or not at the end of the session as I did not have a spider with me! (I believe that is a method used in another type of therapy.) I simply asked Anna to let me know how she felt when she next saw a spider. This is the text I received:

'I had been hoovering my kitchen. Out crawled a huge spider with a body!!!! I did not scream, I did not jump and I calmly picked it up with a glass and a plate and put it outside!!!! Eeeeeek!!!!! I was scared but not much; I felt sorry for it more than anything! All while my son was watching me!! X'

She was so pleased that she did a testimonial for my website to encourage others to get help for their phobias.

EFT Testimonial by Anna Noden:

'I had never heard of EFT before Gillian asked me if I wanted to try it for my spider phobia. I have to admit that, when it was first explained to me, I thought it sounded a bit weird. It was not hard to do, or follow. In fact, it was pretty easy really. I had had a spider phobia since the age of about 10 and it affected me every day. I used to be watching for them all the time, under shoes, piles of clothes and stuff, etc. While I was doing the session, it did feel strange at first but then I relaxed and felt quite calm.

The other brilliant thing is that I do not even think about spiders now. It is great not to have that constant worry and fear that one will be there.

I would definitely recommend that you try EFT as it really does work! Gillian explains it clearly and she makes it easy and relaxing to do.'

In an update on Anna's EFT success, nearly 18 months after her session, Anna took this photo herself, totally amazing her family and friends. Her caption was 'How near am I to that spider?'

Anxiety/self-confidence issue

I was contacted via the EFT Register by someone looking for a local practitioner to help them with quite a few issues. Kim had a course of sessions, and worked hard in between them to get great results. Kim's testimonial:

> 'Gillian is fantastic and has made me feel so comfortable in each of our sessions. You can tell that she genuinely cares and wants to help.
>
> I had been battling with issues of anxiety and lack of self-confidence/self-belief (affecting my work as a medical professional in the NHS and relationships) for several years and I had had limited success with Cognitive Behavioural Therapy (CBT) and hypnosis. I first became aware of Emotional Freedom Technique (EFT) when my partner told me that she had had it in the past for similar issues and it had worked for her. I looked for an EFT Practitioner near where I lived and came across Gillian.
>
> Gillian is wonderful! She is very warm and friendly and easy to work with. She explained the EFT process clearly and always explains what she is doing. Although I still have a lot of work to do, EFT has had an enormous effect on my life. I leave sessions with Gillian feeling more positive, confident and calm. Gillian also explains what I can do at home, between sessions, and gives me exercises that I can do to continue the healing process.
>
> I would highly recommend Gillian and EFT.'

Cluster headaches

Derek was introduced to EFT through his wife. He was open to it and extremely grateful for the effect it had on his life. This is his testimonial:

'I had never heard of EFT before and when it was first explained to me, I thought it sounded very interesting!

I had been struggling with cluster headaches for 40 years and they were very disruptive at times.

I found it easy to do and felt positive about it even in my first session.

I have used EFT with great success at home on numerous occasions, even using it while in public (in the pub for example). When my cluster headaches start, there is no time to worry what others might think. The important thing is to treat it there and then just as you might with tablets!

EFT was a success for me, it sped up the rate at which the headache disappeared and, after 40 years of suffering, my cluster headaches are now under control.

I would recommend EFT to others without a doubt and most certainly recommend Gillian and thank her for all her help.'

Blushing issues

KH picked up one of my leaflets at a local beauty salon and rang me to see if I could help with her blushing issue. She was amazed and extremely happy with the results.

'I had never heard of EFT until I came across one of Gillian's leaflets. I read through it and thought I would give it a go as the counselling I had been having was not helping my problems.

I chose EFT to help with anxiety and blushing as it was affecting the quality of my life.

Every day, I felt exhausted from trying to avoid situations that would make me blush. I would blush at any moment and it made me feel silly and withdrawn from the world around me.

After only three visits to Gillian, I felt like a new person, I had not blushed once since starting the sessions and my confidence and outlook on life were fantastic.

Gillian's sessions are easy to follow. I found them very relaxing and I even managed to carry on doing EFT at home.

Thanks to Gillian and EFT, I can carry on knowing that if I feel a little anxious, I can take a few moments and perform EFT easily. I would recommend it to anyone! Thanks again.'

PTSD

One client, who for personal reasons does not wish to be identified, said the following:

'I came to Gillian with feelings of lack of self-worth (I had been told I had PND and PTSD). I had previously had CBT, but felt that I had hit a wall with it and that it was no longer helping.

EFT has helped me so much. I come away from each session feeling refreshed and have a more positive outlook on the trials and feelings that I am facing.

I cannot recommend EFT enough. I think that everyone can benefit from it somehow.

I love that it is something you can practise at home alone in-between sessions.'

Tapping Circles

I have the privilege of running Tapping Circles where I teach people how to tap in a group environment. First, I explain a bit about the history of EFT. Next, I teach them the tapping sequence and do a demonstration. The group then discusses and decides what issue we will work on. Someone approached me to see if I could help them and their children who were having a very difficult time, and they wondered if I could help them with any stress-relief type classes for children and parents. The client and children were in a very emotional state. The children had been having counselling at school, which didn't seem to be helping and so they wondered if I did any sort of therapy sessions that they could attend to help them with their anger and anxiety. I suggested that they learn EFT and the parent came for a session first to see what it was about and if they thought it would benefit the children. The session went well and they decided to have some 'Family Tapping Circles'. This was amazing and the children really enjoyed it. I taught them how to do 'private' tapping to use in difficult situations so people would not know what they were doing but it would help them to cope and feel better.

The feedback was great, some of the children said that they had used it at school to help them cope. At one of the sessions, a grandparent came with them as they too had been affected by the experiences and was eager to help the family cope. It was a real honour to tap with three generations and teach the family a tool to help them in everyday life. What price can you put on learning to be emotionally literate? This is truly a life-changing technique at your fingertips!

My wish is that more children and families could learn this wonderful technique and use it to be their best selves. How wonderful would that be? This is something that I am going to pursue in the future, offering family tapping circles for those in crisis or difficulty.

I will also be working with other EFT practitioners, approaching schools and colleges to offer them the opportunity for their students to learn and benefit from this technique. It really is for *EVERYONE!*

EFT: For you and me ... and everyone

by Dulcie Williams

My journey to EFT

I first experienced EFT in the 1990s after yet another failed diet. I went to see an EFT practitioner who helped me lose all interest in chocolate! Amazing but true. Weirdly I never went back. I do not think I could afford it at the time but it always stayed with me. Years later, I learned to do it myself from Gary Craig's website. Oddly, I only used it in emergencies despite his plea to try it on everything. The time must not have been right for me just then.

From 2012 to 2014, I started reading more and decided to train to become a practitioner. I had no real plans to run a practice: rather to help family, friends and myself. I had a strange feeling I would be good at it, and I am. Gillian is better!

I really needed stress management, having had some huge life challenges: childhood abuse, illness, death of family members, losing my home after my husband's business collapsed and almost losing our marriage. I really needed and wanted to clear away the associated stress, resentment and grief. EFT seemed a better option than drugs or drink.

On one of the training courses I attended, I met Gillian Morris, the author of this book. I generally like most people I meet but, when I worked with Gillian, her humour, warmth and skill were immediately evident. She is a woman of integrity. She was very skilled at EFT and more than anything she truly listened to me, using my own words and specific responses in our tapping sessions to help me clear a lot of deep-seated emotional pain.

On that particular course, I had the amazing experience of helping another trainee clear a huge phobia of motorways. She drove home the next day on the motorway. So I was already thrilled with the course, with EFT and quite frankly, with myself. Half an hour later, in another classroom session, I was shocked to find myself opening up to Gillian about my own childhood abuse. I had hardly dared to speak to anyone about these things. I had spoken to NSPCC years before but that had not helped so I assumed I was stuck with my hideous half memories forever. For some reason, I just decided to trust her and tap away all that pain, shame and confusion.

I imagine Gillian will be embarrassed that I am writing about her because she is a very humble and reserved person. However, I owe her and EFT a huge debt of gratitude for getting my head and heart clear of that heavy burden which I had lugged around with me for almost 60 years.

I do not wish to divulge too much of my history but I hope you get an idea of how momentous this EFT session was.

Since then, Gillian and I have worked together on weekly 'Buddy Sessions' via Skype where we tap together on whatever issues are presenting for us at the time. We use a mixture of techniques, one called Tap and Talk and another called Choices, and sometimes make up our own rules. Without exception, we both leave our sessions feeling one hundred per cent better than when we started, even when we do not think we have much to stress over.

A month after my diagnosis of breast cancer, I had a full mastectomy. I am convinced I would not have been able to cope with the emotional and physical trauma as well as I have without my weekly EFT Skype sessions and without the regular tapping in between.

I did vaguely wonder what the hospital staff thought of my tapping routine just before I went to theatre and as I came round in the recovery room.

I can tell you I am finding 'doing cancer' very traumatic. I will not pretend that it is easy. It is the worst thing I have ever had to face other than my children being in pain. EFT is helping me to deal with the shock of my cancer diagnosis, which has completely shaken my foundations. It is hard of course but I know I will grow and flourish, and whatever the outcome, the journey has become much more bearable and often I have happy times and lots of laughter. I am planning to be Gillian's Tapping Buddy for at least another twenty years!

I am no expert in EFT but here is just a list of how EFT has helped me, my family, and my friends:

- Child-abuse trauma cleared;
- Confidence for public speaking;
- Learning to say no, speak up for myself, challenge unkind remarks;
- Confidence for singing in front of 2,000 people (still scary but doable);
- Helping others deal with fear, stress, pain, panic, bereavement, depression, job interviews, fear of driving on motorways, IBS, stage fright and facing a frightening diagnosis;
- Helping children and new mums not to panic and to calm down really quickly after falls, accidents, high temperatures and bullying;
- Confidence to challenge medics and question cancer treatment and options;
- Courage to take treatments which terrify me;
- Courage to look Death right in the eye, cry and carry on.

I do truly believe that EFT is for everyone. However, it is not for those who need it. It is really for those who WANT it. I want it, I use it, and I hope you want it too. It can change your life for the better. It really can.

I hope Gillian's book does what she truly wants; and that is to spread the word and share the incredible benefits EFT has to offer everyone who wants it.

EFT: For empowering adults and children with health concerns

by Dr. Deborah Miller

My journey to EFT

It all began with a teddy bear, a TappyBear to be exact. If you do not know, TappyBear is a stuffed teddy bear with all the tapping points on his body. I had just received my TappyBear and was excited about using him with children.

The very next day, I helped out at a fundraiser for children with cancer. I tapped with five children and met with the head oncologist. It was a life-changing event; one that activated in me a passion to help children and their families deal with the emotions that arise when a child has a serious illness.

That day also inspired me to go to the hospital daily to tap with the children. I was so touched by the experience: how it helped everyone feel better and even more so by what I received. Those brave souls inspired me to help people learn how to use tapping as a tool for creating a healthier life and lifestyle.

I learned so much about the needs of the children, their parents, family members, the nurses and medical staff, that I felt compelled to write the book *The Dragon with Flames of Love*. I knew this book had to be more than just stories about children with cancer, so I wrote it as a manual and guide to using tapping to help improve the quality of life of those in that difficult situation.

Case Studies

Real life experiences - Mary

The first thing you notice about Mary is her big smile. It stretches across her face and lights up the room. She generally has that cheerful smile and did so even after she had surgery to remove an abdominal tumour.

Tummy talk

Tapping with Mary is always fun because children do not need all the words that adults do. In addition, many children cannot explain what emotions they feel or describe their fears or discomfort in words. Since children are visual (i.e. they love images and stories), we used images instead. We did what I called 'tummy talk', since her tummy still felt uncomfortable after the surgery. Mary wanted her tummy to feel better.

We chose to send a lot of love to her tummy. I asked her what colour love would look like. She said that love was red: red like the colour of a tomato. We tapped while imagining sending 'red-like-a-tomato' love to her tummy. She giggled since she liked the image very much.

Visualizing while tapping helped Mary laugh, relax and have a distinct image of her tummy getting better and feeling loved. Doing so allowed her to be positive, which in turn sent a message to her body to initiate a healing response, which her body naturally knows how to do. She was helping her body along by being a positive influence.

Hair loss

Losing your hair due to chemotherapy is a traumatic experience for child and adult alike. One day, I wanted to take a picture of Mary, but she did not want me to because she had lost all of her hair.

I asked her where beauty came from. She did not know. I told her it came from inside and that she was always beautiful. We tapped about beauty coming from the inside and that its outward expression was her smiles and giggles. She liked that a lot. After tapping, she felt beautiful no matter what. From that point on she was willing to have her photo taken, regardless of whether or not she had hair.

Bone-marrow transplant

Mary was scheduled for a bone-marrow transplant but the idea of it scared her. We tapped on what it entailed. Then we tapped to reduce her fears and worries. Finally, we tapped about the outcome she desired. As she tapped, she felt more and more positive about the procedure. She came to the point where she chose to get better. She was willing to do whatever was necessary for her to do so. This included tapping to reduce the stress in her body, to eliminate her fears and doubts, and to instil in her body the image of it being completely well and vibrantly healthy.

Since we are all individuals, each person has his or her own course of action that can lead to recovery and maintaining one's health. Tapping has helped Mary create a healthier environment for her recovery, which includes tapping, allopathic treatments, a bone-marrow transplant, as well as wiser dietary choices.

A side benefit of Mary's tapping routine is how it affected her mother; a sweet woman who is quite anxious a good portion of the time. Mary reminds her mum to tap with her at night and that helps her mother be calmer and more focused too. It also creates quality time spent together feeling calm and happy.

Overall, Mary's learning to tap has allowed her to think positive thoughts and feel happy. That has had a positive effect on her immune response. Thus, tapping has empowered Mary in her healing process and that is a tremendous benefit.

David

When I first met David, he was only 2 years and 8 months old. He was full of energy but also angry. He was angry and grumpy about being in the hospital, about his treatments, about the pain and about being sick. At first, he resisted tapping, but as I surrogate tapped for him he relaxed and even his voice softened. Afterwards, David was happy to tap with me.

Tapping with Deborah

One day we sat in the playroom on little orange chairs (funny how we remember those small details). We tapped together, with him mimicking the points I tapped on and the tapping phrases I used. I like to make tapping fun so I would add funny little phrases as well as confidence-building phrases like 'I am a good boy. I am smart. I want to get better'.

He enjoyed this simple tapping session about how wonderful he was and that he deserved to get better. When we finished, he was happy and he told me his body felt good too. This is an important aspect of the recovery process. Feeling good helps the immune system do its repair functions.

Tapping on his own

David's mother watched David use tapping when he was angry. She was amazed at how well he used tapping and how quickly his anger dissipated. She told me that David was angry and upset but instead of yelling, crying or having a temper tantrum he began to tap something along these lines: 'Even though I am mad, I am a good boy. Even though I am angry, I am a great kid.' Then he tapped through the tapping points. After two rounds, he stopped and went off to play calmly: his anger was gone.

We do not know the exact words David used but the important aspect is that he had the wisdom to use tapping to get rid of his anger. He did not need to know the history of tapping or the science behind it. His mother did not have to do anything to help him. He did not even need to know the art behind the wording (which worries so many of us adults – what are the RIGHT words or the MAGIC words). He just tapped, his anger went away and he went back to playing.

He did it all on his own, of his own volition. That is why I love tapping. It allows children as young as David, 3 years old at the time, to manage their own emotions. That is an empowered child, and that is a true gift.

As David got older, he started to tap any time he was scheduled to have a spinal tap, a painful procedure for any child. David would tap before and after the procedure. His parents did not tell him to tap. He knew from experience that if he tapped he was calmer and the pain was less. He was smart enough to apply tapping to feel better. He did not need to be reminded.

He also taps when he gets itchy from one particular medication. He taps and as he told me: 'the itching goes away.' Most likely, this occurs because tapping reduces stress and inflammatory hormones in the body.

David's initiative to tap inspired his parents to begin tapping along with their son and on their own. That creates a delightful connection and a healthier atmosphere between them all.

I find it endearing that children who use tapping to feel better inspire their parents to tap too.

Nurses and medical staff

The workload and emotional strain of being in charge of the health of those in your care is very stressful. Most nurses and medical staff carry that stress with them every day. They have little time to take care of themselves. Tapping is an easy, quick and practical way that they can reduce their stress load so that they can think more clearly, and calmly do their job well.

This may seem obvious, but it is an important aspect of supporting those who are ill: taking care of the caretakers. They have great needs too. In individual and group tapping sessions, I've been touched as I watch them release the stress of seeing pain and suffering every day.

The Future

The field of Cellular Biology claims that less than 2% of ALL disease is genetic. This means that 98% of ALL disease is preventable through lifestyle and health design.
Dr Bruce Lipton, *The Wisdom of your Cells.*

This statement gives us so much hope to prevent and manage disease. In my experience, there are three key requirements to creating health:

1. Detoxify your physical body;
2. Nourish your physical body and its immune system;
3. Manage your thoughts and feelings.

This third point is probably the most important since epigenetics shows that the environment determines if and how a gene is expressed. That environment is determined by all of one's feelings and emotions (both positive and negative). Thus, the emotional environment influences the behaviours and reactions one has, which in turn develop into one's habits. In order to create health, one has to eliminate negative feelings, toxic thoughts and memories of childhood traumas and instil in their place positive, peaceful and loving emotions.

With tapping, we can manage those emotions so that we no longer need to be victims of our past traumas and experiences. We can free ourselves from them, and in turn free our body from 'dis-ease'.

Let us take back our power and manage our health instead of waiting for disease to arrive. Our bodies are self-healing: i.e. the cells in our bodies do everything in their power to be healthy. If you give your body a little help – by detoxifying and nourishing your body, and healing your emotional traumas and unhealthy childhood beliefs, your body will do its best to be healthy.

My desire is to help people feel empowered and capable of maintaining a healthy state of mind and body. I would like to create a world where children (and adults) tap daily to feel calm and relaxed, to release their traumas and in turn, excel because they are free to believe in themselves. Now wouldn't that be a blessing to the world?

EFT: In groups (borrowing benefits)

by Tania Aranda

My journey to EFT

In 2011, I found myself giving birth to my beautiful second boy and also losing my job, which had brought me to Belgium eight years earlier. How I can best describe that period is as a rollercoaster of emotions. Too many things were happening at the same time, so many of them out of my control. I was feeling overwhelmed, as I could not keep my past life, which was unravelling before my eyes. I was taken over by an immense sadness, provoked by the loss of my job and what it represented to me: the loss of security. I was losing the life I had worked hard to build up over the last eight years in this country. It appeared to vanish in a matter of months.

I was frozen in fear and physically exhausted. I was afraid of the future, the unknown, the changes and new challenges waiting to be tackled. I recognized that I was running on empty batteries – not knowing what to do, or how to deal with the life-changing events at that time made me feel desperate because I could not see clearly and did not know what I wanted. All of this was happening while trying to raise a toddler and a newborn baby. I felt lonely (I had never missed my family that much), overwhelmed and with no wish or energy to think about incorporating myself into the work force. The thought of going back to work only produced anxiety and a big fear of being incapable of coping with family and a full-time job as I had in the past.

I did not really understand why I was feeling the way I was. It was so difficult to communicate on any level with my husband. I felt misunderstood and he felt betrayed. Who was this woman? Definitely not the one he had married. We began to wonder if we were meant to be together. I am not going to get in to the details but if you have ever heard about 'couple crisis' – we were there.

Back then, I believed that staying in Belgium was the 'mother creator' of all my problems. 'It must be the weather', I used to think. 'It is so cold and I don't know how to cope and live in these rough conditions.' (I seemed to have forgotten that I had coped with it for 8 years, with the normal ups and downs from not having everyday sun as I was used to.) I was convinced that moving back to Mexico and ending my marriage was the solution to my problems. All I wanted was to pack my stuff, take my kids and fly away, no matter what the consequences would have been. I obviously was not thinking straight and was convinced running away was the solution to my problems.

I started therapy with a psychologist on the recommendation of my gynecologist who had diagnosed me with post-partum depression. I only saw her for a couple of months, once a week, but it did not really change the way I was feeling. Luckily, a good friend suggested I take a look at alternative therapy. In my desperation, I went to the first person

I found on the Internet, who suggested something to do with Chinese acupressure. I did not understand what it was but I went anyway.

As you can imagine, I had a head full of emotions and, like in the cartoons, I felt I carried a grey cloud wherever I went. I do not remember much about the first tapping session, but what I do remember is how I felt at the end of it: like a weight had lifted from my shoulders. I felt content for the first time in a while and, while I was walking out of the practice, I noticed how the light was touching the leaves and that there were birds singing. This was the same place I had been an hour and a half earlier when it had looked grey and rainy (remember I carried my cloud everywhere) and I certainly did not hear the birds singing. Something had happened! The way I saw my surroundings had changed as had my internal perspective of the situation. It was not that the light, the trees and the birds singing were not there before; I was just unable to notice them while I was so disconnected from my body and my energy system. I was so out of balance; I could not enjoy or notice the beauty around me.

With EFT, I started releasing, bit by bit, the years of unresolved emotions. Today, I am glad I decided to clear past events connected to negative emotions. I know EFT has helped me to transform my life in to the shape that I want. EFT is a marvelous tool that has profoundly affected the way I deal with the past, but most exciting is how I shape and tackle my present. It has been a wonderful recovery and transformational journey.

Everyone experiences the blues, depression, sadness, grief anxiety and other negative emotions. We are just human beings dealing with a great variety of emotions which work as stop lights. Experiencing negative emotions is an indicator of an imbalance in our energy system. When it happens, it is like having a bottleneck in your energy system, preventing the normal flow of energy. With these emotions, your body is communicating with you, alerting you to the fact that there is something bothering you, which you need to address and resolve. Positive emotions like joy, appreciation, enthusiasm, peace, gratitude and excitement are there to confirm that what we are doing can only be good for us, and therefore worth pursuing and maintaining that emotional state with the same kind of thoughts and actions. It is a way of trying to ensure a happier stay on this planet.

One night during a group tapping session I had one of those 'aha' moments. Finally, I had found clarity, and as I listened to myself, I felt this deep desire to do something related to tapping, to teach and spread the benefits of this wonderful tool. One can heal from whatever we are distressed about. We no longer need to suffer! With tapping, we can easily help our body release its natural ability to heal. We are just naïve, but once we learn about it, it is there with us for the rest of our lives. It is my objective to introduce and support my clients to open up to the possibilities of self-healing, so that they, too, can have the ride of their life.

Case studies

Group sessions – borrowing benefits

I really enjoy group sessions. Why? Because I can reach more people at once. The participants do not have to be 100 per cent tuned in during the session to their personal problem. This allows them to release their negative emotions and work around the problem in a very gentle way. It creates empathy. People become aware that we share the same worries, concerns and sometimes pain. It provides a supportive, caring and safe environment in which they can let go of their problems. The group's energy also helps the volunteer and themselves to heal faster. Why? This is one of the reasons it fascinates me – because we are all one. As Albert Einstein said: 'everything is a big energy field'. When I tap on myself, the frequency vibrations reach other people and when you have a group of people tapping at the same time, the vibrations are multiplied and therefore stronger than when doing it alone. Isn't that great?

I use group sessions in two scenarios: the first one is when I want to invite new people to the world of tapping. I organize what I call my Tupperware-tapping events. I normally ask friends or people who have worked with me doing tapping, to help me organize a tapping demo. Then we pick up a topic that will be of interest to the crowd. I normally offer the following topics: how to improve relationships or how to reduce stress. I find most people identify with one or the other.

The idea of the demonstration is for me to show how, by applying EFT, it is possible to release problems in a gentle and respectful way, in front of an audience where all the participants can obtain benefits by tapping along. It is always crucial to protect the privacy and safety of the client. Depending on the issue, it is essential to mention that we might not be able to cover the whole problem but that we can reduce at least some of its intensity.

After I give a brief introduction about EFT and explain the meridian points, I proceed with the tapping demonstration to the group.

In one of the demonstrations, where the topic was 'how to improve relationships', I asked, 'who has a person in mind that is creating any type of negative emotions and would like to feel at ease and calm next time you see him/her?' Normally, people can identify a person who gets on their nerves, or find something about them that makes them uncomfortable. I ask them to pick ONLY one person in their minds, as EFT works with specifics and we cannot manage more than one difficult person at a time.

Annie volunteered one night. I explained that I did not need to know who that person was, she only had to share what emotion this person evoked in her. We worked on the confusion of her emotions towards her person: love and hate.

'Even though it is so confusing to love this person, sometimes I hate him too, I love and approve of me and how I feel.'

'Even though sometimes I think I hate him and I love him at the same time – it is so confusing – I love and accept how I feel right now.'

'Even though my emotions are in conflict, I have these love and hate feelings for this person, I love, forgive and accept how I feel about this conflict.'

Annie had a Subjective Units of Distress (SUD) of 10 in her chest. Not long after starting, she began to cry quietly. I immediately went to the trauma points, (wrist and under the nose) there was no need to say any words. Instead, I focused on her breathing and assured her how well she was doing. At the same time, I also told her that we were all there for her, that it was all okay and that she was doing great. We did a few rounds until Annie started to calm down and her expression returned to normal. I asked her how she was feeling and if she wanted to do one more round of tapping, to which she said yes, so we proceeded with a very general statement.

'Even though I have this internal conflict related to this person, I love and accept myself completely.'

'Even though I have this conflict and I don't know what to do, I choose to calm down. I am doing the best I can right now.'

'Even though I don't know what to do with this conflict, I choose to know I am handling it to the best of my abilities.'

We did a few rounds pointing at the conflict; and we tried to address how confusing it was for her to have two opposite emotions at the same time for one person. We continued until she started to be more at ease, her body and facial expression were relaxed and her SUD dropped to 5.

This issue with her person needed more work, but considering this was a group session I could not address the core issues there. I explained: 'this is as far as we can go now, but if you want, we could continue during a separate meeting.' For the time being, I asked her to focus on her person while we tapped on the following participant as she could still benefit from the next round.

Annie decided to work on this and other emotional issues related to her, for example, her weight problem. We worked together for twelve sessions and tackled different emotional aspects relating to weight which were affecting other areas of her life, like work and her personal relationship with her partner. I spoke to her recently and she shared some really wonderful news:

She is now moving to a different country and consolidating her love relationship (this is a big success for her, as I know how much it means to her to take the next step in the relationship);

She is focused on having a good routine: walking, going to the gym and dancing;

She is working on her personal inspirational project as a photographer;

She is also looking for a new job and learning the language of the country to where she will move;

She is handling all the changes in her life in a much more controlled way;

She has lost 4 kg.

Even though her transformational process is still in the early stages, she has had some wonderful breakthroughs of love and self-acceptance. I am confident that in her own time she will achieve all her goals and desires.

A Program created for group tapping

The second scenario is for specific themes which are designed to tackle a much bigger topic, broken down into several related sub-topics, forming a program. This program consists of several group sessions of two hours each, where participants are asked to tune in with a specific issue related to a particular negative belief.

I have reproduced a program created by my dear coach and mentor Jeanine Crombe to 'eliminate core negative beliefs around wealth'.

The topics covered in this weekly program are:

Procrastination: I know I have to do it, part of me wants to and another part of me is holding me back. I am anxious, nervous, I feel so guilty for postponing the inevitable. I feel incapable. What if it is not good enough? I am protecting myself from a big fear of failure. I'd rather do nothing than embarrass myself;

Guilt: for having more or wishing for more: How can I ask for more if others are in need? I feel guilty already. I have had more opportunities than others. It feels like I am taking advantage of others who need it more than I do;

<u>I am afraid to stand out</u>: It is absolutely not safe for me to shine; I will hurt some people. I know more than a couple of bad things that will happen if I excel. You cannot have it all. My family, friends or colleagues will not love or accept me; I will not be like them;

<u>My vibration (feeling) about money is more about the absence of it</u>: I do not possess anywhere near as much money as I would like. I feel fear and disappointment with regards to my lack of money. I am struggling with my financial situation. I am anxious, angry and frustrated about my finances. It is not fair. I deserve more! What is prosperity? Whatever it is, it is not for me. I am living proof that there is not enough. Scarcity is all I see. Generating money is such a struggle. I feel really sad. I do not deserve abundance and success. Reality is that you must work hard to make a month-end;

<u>My negative beliefs about rich people</u>: They are ungracious and greedy. I envy them for what they have. It is not fair that they have so much and I so little. Where is the equal distribution of wealth? Deep inside me, I do not want to become like them. If I become prosperous, I will become all the terrible things I believe about prosperous people;

<u>It is safer to stay where I am</u>: I feel safe in my comfort zone. I do not want to take on more responsibilities. I will not have free time. I fear being successful and the things that it will bring: more responsibility,

status, money, etc. What if I fail? It would hurt too much to fall from higher. I would rather stay in my comfort zone than be successful. It is too much work.

During each session, we tackle the different angles of each issue. I provide a brief introduction about the problem, make targeted questions related to the topic and ask the participants to tune in with whatever issue they choose to work on at the time. I ask them to create a title of their movie ("the movie" is a technique used in EFT. You think of the issue or problem and run the memory/movie in your mind whilst tapping on the issue), and ask them to park it in the back of their mind. I then proceed to work with a volunteer, targeting their chosen problem, and we all tap together for that person. The participants are releasing their own topic in their subconscious mind at the same time.

Here are some of the comments I received after the workshop:

'I did not know EFT before I met Tania. The technique surprised me and I marveled at Tania's ability to devote the time to find the emotions and ideas that I usually hide pretty well. I took the course with my partner, friend and sister and, ever since, there is a before and after: improving our relationship, improving us as a team. Personally, I have experienced a process of awakening memories of bad experiences, of limiting processed thoughts that I was not aware of and have decided to take on the task of redefining them and restructuring ideas to advance. Always grateful.' *Monica Verdi, Barcelona*.

'I knew nothing about EFT before I met Tania. The technique amazed me from the first session, from observing how emotions change. The sessions with Tania have always been useful and fun. I think she is a very intuitive and human person. The greatest blessing is to see that my work relationship with my partner has changed thanks to EFT. We now work more efficiently and harmoniously without wasting time discussing our emotional power. Thanks dear Tania!' *Jessica Verdi, Brussels.*

'The EFT group sessions brought me something new and extremely positive. The themes were of general interest and each individual contributed with her own experience. I would recommend this excellent therapy.' *Ivonne Araujo, Brussels***.**

The future

The more I learn and understand about the power of tapping, the more excited I get from knowing such a potent self-healing tool, and the bigger my desire is to master, excel and share my expertise and life experience with as many people as possible. This tool has transformed 'me' into 'ME'. There could be no greater joy or happiness than the self-discovery of the wonderful person I had forgotten to be. Our essence is there, thanks to God, or the highest being or whatever you want to call it. 'It' never leaves us. With tapping, it is possible to dig deep and remove unnecessary scars, and the more we tap and clean the emotional waste, the more we find the treasure that lies within us.

I work with clients who are going through challenging times in their lives and support them through those changes smoothly and successfully.

I especially love working with people who want to reach a higher level of consciousness and are ready to explore and learn from their inner selves so they can, first, feel joyful by loving and accepting who they are, and second, connect with their deep desires and accomplish success as they define it.

EFT: For workplace stress

by Gill Pinnington

My journey to EFT

Stress: a catalyst for change

It was back in 2006 when I first became interested in workplace stress and interventions for dealing with it. I had moved from Oxford to Eastbourne and as I secured a role supporting a head of department and five managers in a large educational institution, I found myself with not only a change of view but of workplace culture too. Having worked in management roles in the private sector, where stress was commonplace, it was a real surprise to discover that management, support and curriculum teams in the public sector experienced increasing levels of stress. Having to do more with less took its toll on everyone and workplace stress-related absences were rising, as was presenteeism; colleagues at all levels were going off sick or continuing to work when they should have been at home.

This could easily have gone unnoticed by me but for two factors: I had become aware of my own rising stress levels; and an opportunity arose for me to carry out a research project on interventions for dealing with workplace stress. My role in the organisation was interesting and engaging. I had control over my workload and I was surrounded by an incredibly supportive team, yet I had no strategy for coping with what life was throwing up and I keenly felt the impact of even the smallest of workplace stressors. I appeared not to be alone in this.

I progressed within the organization and later found myself at a point where I knew I had to seek support. I had gone beyond stress and anxiety, and was living with full-blown depression. I had a great boss, worked in a supportive team and in an organization that valued and supported diversity, yet I found it so difficult to speak about what I was going through. It was the hardest thing in the world, what would people say and think? I was imprisoned within the four walls of stigma, shame, guilt and fear: stigma of being labelled, shame of not being 'strong enough' to cope, guilt about letting down colleagues and students, and fear of being 'found out' and losing my job in the next round of cuts.

I was stressed, depressed and incredibly unhappy. It felt like I was in a deep, dark hole with no hope of escape. Eventually, I confided in a friend and colleague who recommended a local psychotherapist with an excellent reputation – it turned out to be the most important conversation of my life. It led to me sitting here now, writing this chapter.

After several months of weekly psychotherapy, my mood was improving but I still found myself on an emotional roller coaster. My therapist asked if I had heard about EFT tapping and how it could help me to manage my feelings. Like so many, I had bought a book on EFT only to let it gather dust. I was keen to try and, in those early days of tapping, it was a true revelation; not only did it help me to move forward in sessions, it gave me a tool to use in-between. No longer was I a passenger in my own life. Instead, I was learning how to be the pilot. Having a tool to identify and transform the emotions hiding beneath the umbrella of stress and anxiety was truly liberating. I was free at last.

Three years later, I finished those precious weekly sessions and, with the full support and encouragement of my psychotherapist, I embarked on the next stage of my journey; becoming an EFT and Matrix Reimprinting practitioner.

The impact of stress and anxiety in the workplace

In the 10 years since my initial interest in workplace stress, and having come through a tough recession with continued year-on-year cuts in both public and private sector organizations, it is a rare individual, at any level, who has not felt the hot hands of stress touch their collar. And it would appear that the problem is not going away.

Data collected by the Health and Safety Executive from THOR-GP and the Labour Force Survey show that the prevalence of work-related stress, anxiety and depression has been consistent for 10 years. In 2014/15, it accounted for 35 per cent of all work-related ill health cases and 43 per cent of all working days lost due to ill health – a staggering 9.9 million days in the UK alone. The likelihood of this happening to you increases with the size of your organization, industry and occupation. Employees in health and social work, education, public administration and defence have 'statistically significantly higher prevalence rates compared with all industries'. However, private sector organizations are also significantly affected.

If you want more proof, the Absence Management 2015 annual report, undertaken by the Chartered Institute of Personnel and Development in partnership with Simply Health, found that 41 per cent of organizations saw an increase in mental health issues such as depression and anxiety in the previous 12 months. This fully supports anecdotal evidence from friends, ex-colleagues and business associates, as well as from the clients that I work with.

With mental ill health costing UK businesses, a colossal £26 billion each year, absenteeism at consistently high levels and a 31 per cent increase in presenteeism, one thing is clear: something must change.

Case study

Creating resilient teams

Resilience, being able to bounce back from adversity, conflict and failure, is the key to reducing, overcoming and, to some extent, preventing the prevalence of workplace stress, anxiety and depression.

Any person living with stress, anxiety or depression will tell you of its detrimental effect upon health and wellbeing. When whole teams are affected, the effects are not limited to the individuals but magnified, rippling out through all areas of the business, thus affecting morale, motivation, productivity, employee turnover, profits and even business reputation.

There is evidence from Seymour & Grove (2005) to show that taking simple steps to promote and improve wellbeing, including a range of stress management interventions, is the best way to prevent this from happening, especially when focused at an individual level.

Modern pressures on businesses of all sizes will remain, so it is vital that each individual develops a Personal Resilience Toolkit to help them navigate the storms and squalls of life. Furthermore, when managers and their teams, at every level of an organization, are encouraged to support each other openly and share experiences, the walls of stigma, shame, guilt and fear start to crumble. Forward-thinking conscious businesses who invest in their most valuable asset, their staff, are the ones who adopt such strategies.

Recently, I had the opportunity to work with a small business with a reputation for putting people at the heart of what they do. As in many organisations, staffing had been reduced so workloads had somewhat increased. They invested in their people and had organisational and team values. Their goals were realistic and there was great cohesion within the team, yet several employees experienced high levels of stress, some with extended periods of absence. This created a significant strain on individuals, the team and the business as a whole. What they needed were practical ways to reduce stress, manage emotions and build resilience.

Several team members, including a manager, were experiencing many of the common effects of stress and anxiety, namely, poor decision making and problem solving, confusion, brain fog, decreased productivity, increased mistakes and a loss of patience with each other and their clients. Physical health was also suffering with more colds and bugs and lower energy levels, poor sleep quality and increased tiredness. In addition to this, some found that, in this state, they made poor food choices, were less likely to get outside at lunchtime and had reduced or stopped exercising because they were so tired.

With EFT at its core, my Building Resilience workshop combined effective and empowering practical techniques with essential knowledge about stress and resilience. When I explained about the practical tools they were going to use, there was a mixed reaction. Some were happy to have a go even though the activities were a little 'unusual', others were reluctant, even resistant, to try something new. However, one thing they all agreed upon was that it would be useful in both their personal and business life to be more able to cope with stress and gain control of how they felt.

After discussing how stress and anxiety are 'umbrellas', sheltering a host of difficult emotions, the group then used the highly effective Stress Target to identify their major stress triggers and the resulting negative thoughts (or limiting beliefs) and emotions. Even before we had started tapping, several of the group had some big 'aha' moments as they saw patterns of thinking and emotions emerge. Jane commented, 'I had no idea of the extent to which my thoughts and emotions were linked; it is great to recognize this and know that I will be able to do something about it.'

Then followed an EFT demonstration with John, one of the managers working on a current major stressor he had identified using the Stress

Target. Having a manager take the lead gave the group more confidence. Even the sceptics were taking interest. Fifteen minutes later, everyone could see the difference it had made to John; not only that, they had had a taste of it themselves through group tapping and 'borrowing benefits'.

When asked about the experience, John said, 'It was a shock to realise I was feeling so angry and frustrated about the situation and how it was fuelling the stress that I was feeling. I cannot remember the last time I felt calm and relaxed; it is corny but I feel like I have a new lease of life. I will definitely have a go on my own.'

Thirty minutes later, after more group tapping, each member of the group had experienced their own personal shifts, and was feeling quite confident that they could do it alone. Mary, who at the start had been resistant, shared with the group: 'now I am used to it, it is actually quite easy and I am impressed with the results. It is so empowering to know I can change how I feel within a few minutes then get on with my day without feeling rubbish.'

By the end of the workshop, there was renewed energy and focus within the group and a common desire to make use of EFT and the other great tools that made up their Personal Resilience Toolkit. Collectively, they decided upon and signed up to a simple wellbeing charter. They committed themselves to individual and team support and a new way of working together to promote and celebrate positive emotional health and increased resilience.

The future

It is clear to see that the cost and the effects of stress, anxiety and depression are significant at individual, team and organizational levels. Yet, what if it does not have to be that way?

What if we could create a happier, healthier workforce? A workforce which bounces back from setbacks, is able to influence how it feels, so it can work at optimal levels even under pressure, while experiencing increased personal and business success, wouldn't that be amazing?

I believe wholeheartedly that businesses that invest time, energy and budget in training individuals to develop their own Personal Resilience Toolkit and a commitment to creating a company wellbeing charter will reap rich rewards not only for their bottom line but also for their people, their organisational culture and their reputation.

My belief in EFT as an effective and empowering tool for reducing stress and building resilience remains steadfast, as does my passion for working with businesses of all sizes, creating workplaces that are free from stigma and filled with fully engaged, highly motivated teams who can cope with the demands and pressures of business, while loving what they do. How does it get any better?

EFT: And academic performance

by John Soriano

My journey to EFT

My work with EFT began in 2006. My daughter was having difficulty in middle school, and I was desperate to find something to help her. It was then that I came across a programme called Rediscover the Joy of Learning by Dr Don Blackerby. This was the answer I was looking for then, and is still the fundamental structure I use in my work today.

The programme contained a section on something called EFT, or Emotional Freedom Technique. Dr Blackerby used EFT to help clear school-related traumas in students who were having difficulty learning. I have to admit; I was more than apprehensive when I first came across this. I mean really, changing emotions by tapping on your face? In fact, I was so put off by this, that I actually left this section until the very end of my studies. Wanting to complete my training, I had no choice but to engage with this section of the material. So, with hesitation, I proceeded to work with the material. The rest, as they say, is history.

I could not believe the rapid results I was experiencing, working on my own issues. I became obsessed with EFT and after completing the 'joy of learning' portion, I plunged headlong into studying EFT for its own sake. I earned my advanced certificate of completion for my EFT studies later that year. EFT became exclusively what I was focusing on.

When I launched my private practice, I was still using Dr Blackerby's techniques with my daughter, but was employing EFT to address different issues in my private practice. Unfortunately, Dr Blackerby passed away before I completed my certification and could incorporate his work in education fully into my practice.

After vacillating among a couple of different niches, I decided, on the advice of a good friend and colleague, to come home and focus on the academic applications of EFT. At the time of writing, my primary focus is helping students overcome extreme test anxiety. In addition to this, I use EFT to clear negative beliefs and negative self-image issues as they relate to academic performance. I also use EFT in my work in an urban high school dealing with students with anger and other emotional challenges.

Being able to have a positive impact on the future of our youth by teaching them such a valuable tool as EFT is one of the most rewarding fields of work I can possibly think of.

Case studies

Letiesha

The greatest reward for me is to see the wonderful results I get with students. Take Letiesha for example, a high school senior. In the state of Florida, there is legislation that states that if a senior student has not passed the standardized exam, they cannot graduate with a diploma. This student had been accepted to University in Santa Fe, New Mexico, with a full-ride softball scholarship. The only problem was she had not passed the state standardized exam nor the American College Testing (ACT|). Failure to pass either one of those would have cost her well over $30,000 in scholarship money. As her anxiety grew, her grade on those exams dropped. I met her and asked her to complete a questionnaire to evaluate her levels of test anxiety. On a scale of 1 to 5, she was a 4.5. I talked her through the tapping protocol, and, after just three rounds, her anxiety diminished greatly. After cleaning up some loose ends, she retook the self-assessment test, and scored a 2.5, a significant drop! A few days later, she took another administration of the ACT. After 3 weeks or so, she got her results. Now, due to her ability to stay calm during exams, she had made a five-point swing, and had gone from a 17 to a 22! This made sure she would graduate with a diploma and be able to take advantage of her scholarship.

Another case was Noah.

This student was also a high school senior, and was getting frustrated about his inability to increase his SAT score. He had gone to tutors for test prep but he was still stuck at around the same score. His anxiety was increasing as his confidence was decreasing. As confidence actually sits at higher neurological levels, we took four sessions to clear everything out.

On the day of his exam, he emailed me afterwards and told me how calm he had been during the test and that no matter what happened he was already grateful. A few weeks later, he emailed me to inform me of his 300-point jump on the SAT! Just recently, his father told me that because of the increase in his SAT score, he was accepted by his first-choice university.

Ross

One other example was Ross. This student was also a high school senior and was in danger of not graduating. This student was on and off homeless, with a lot of emotional baggage. He had all but given up on the idea of graduating high school, even though he was highly intelligent. He and I first met in January of that school year, which was to end in mid-May. On paper, he did not have much of a chance. He and I worked after school every day, tapping, and learning more efficient study skills. The tapping was crucial in keeping his head in the game. Because of EFT, he was able to come to me at the end of summer school that year and proudly show me his diploma.

He is also studying psychology in college now, and I wonder sometimes where his life would have been without the magic of EFT. There are hundreds of cases just like these, where EFT changes the direction of young lives forever.

The future

The more work I do in the academic niche, the more I realize how vital the EFT work is in this arena. The rapid growth of standardized testing in just the past two years has led to dramatic increases in school-related stress and anxiety. Statistics show 16 to 20 per cent of all students have extreme test anxiety, with another 18 per cent having moderate test anxiety. This does not include other school-related traumas such as damage to the self-image, bullying, learning disability labels, and more.

I envision my work reaching the countless numbers of learners of all ages who can benefit from it. My mission, a friend of mine even called it my 'ministry', is to change for the better as many lives of struggling learners as I possibly can, both here in the US, and around the world. Through the miracle of technology, such as Skype, I have had the privilege of working with learners worldwide, from New York to Dubai to Australia. Even in full swing, my mission is still just beginning.

EFT: For business confidence

by Lisa Kent

My journey to EFT

I had just started a new job in a busy office, totally thrown in at the deep end. I had to teach myself what to do and how to do it, quickly.

About three months in, I started to feel like I was losing control over my ever-increasing workload. Now don't get me wrong, I like being busy, but this was another level and it was becoming unmanageable. Still being relatively new, I wanted it to look like I was coping but I was steaming through my work without even having time to take in what I was doing. Feeling as though I had make a terrible mistake, I considered my options.

Leaving a job when the going gets too tough is not so simple when you're in your forties. Your CV starts to look like a novel if you are not careful, even with clever editing and a smaller font size, you are not kidding anyone!

I have always been a bit of a control freak, but this felt different. I could feel my heart skipping beats, then adding a few in later for good measure (this is my personal stress indicator – my heart is strong, thank goodness).

I ignored it at first, as it was only happening at work. Imagine my concern when the palpitations lasted all night too. Aware that this was getting out of hand, I spoke to my partner about seeing the doctor and getting something to calm me down. I was confused, withdrawn, and on the verge of becoming depressed.

After frantically searching for an alternative natural therapy to combat how I was feeling, I discovered EFT. At first, I thought it looked ridiculous and even though the science behind it sort of made sense, I was sceptical. I tried it anyway, as I had nothing to lose.

Nothing miraculous happened at first. Although I did calm down generally. After two weeks though, I noticed a shift. I could actually work faster and my brain could keep up and let me think logically about what I was doing; I could prioritize instead of panicking. There was a noticeable difference, subtle, but it was there. I no longer felt completely overwhelmed.

What had changed? Nothing. It had to be the crazy tapping thing!

This was the start of my journey with EFT. I was hooked, so I wanted to find out how I could help others by using this wonderfully simple technique. I found a local trainer and read every book and article I could find on the subject.

Once certified in EFT, I decided to work with people who were suffering from stress in the workplace, as this felt a comfortable place to begin.

Case studies

Workplace stress

Graham came to me experiencing pent up frustration, which he felt was a direct result of his work and other self-esteem issues.

Graham was working with a large financial organisation, in a high-pressured environment where, he told me, people would jump on any and every weakness.

The stress he experienced could be intense at times, with tight deadlines and demanding executives to please. He felt that he needed something to help him not only relieve the pressure of working in this environment, but also to help him with the inevitable effect this was having on his blood pressure and relationships at home.

Although open-minded, Graham had his reservations about working with me and this weird-looking technique. Yes, he had done his YouTube research!

He told me: 'the embarrassment factor was high on the list. What if I got it wrong? Would EFT only suit me if I had "hippy" tendencies? Coupled with the way I was feeling in myself anyway, this all led to me feeling rather apprehensive.'

After around five face-to-face sessions, Graham and I had worked together on a number of different aspects, which had come to light but had not been present or spoken about at the consultation. This often happens with EFT. The stress or 'symptom', which presents itself is often the product of other historic events, traumas and experiences which have carved a path to the place we find ourselves today.

I taught Graham the process of tapping and showed him how to use it discreetly at work or just whenever stress reared its ugly head.

Seven months later, Graham still works at the same company, with new demands and stresses placed on him every day. I asked him to share his progress with me.

'EFT has allowed me to find a way of controlling things in the present. It acts as a great source of comfort in certain situations. I have been able to get into the "zone" and tap my way through scenarios where, historically, I would have become more and more wound up and, ultimately, would have increased my unhappiness in life.

'Although stressful situations still arise, tapping has provided a manageable outlet to keep the blood pressure down and provide myself with a sensible way of remaining in control of some of the curve balls life throws at you – so in this respect I find it very therapeutic.

'Although my technique is probably now slightly diluted, I will use tapping often as a substitute for the traditional "count-to-ten" approach to not "losing it".

'Even when I cannot physically engage in any tapping because of my location and/or the people around me, just thinking about it helps. I have found tapping certain areas over others (such as under the nose and on the collarbone) provides the relief I need to overcome the stress I am experiencing.'

I asked him about his initial reservations with trying something so 'alternative'.

'When I decided to try EFT, paramount in my thoughts was that I needed to embrace this, regardless of the preconceptions I had. I am glad I did!'

Graham's story illustrates the fact that even though we may have no control over the demands placed upon us, what we can do is empower ourselves with the tools to help us stay calm and in a state of mind which keeps us healthier.

In the corporate world, EFT has many applications, as it can reduce stress and increase productivity and creativity.

In America, workplace stress costs the economy an estimated $300 billion every year.

In Britain, 11.4 million workdays are lost due to workplace stress every year.

In France, 30% of suicides happen because of stress at work. Source: www.meettheboss.tv

EFT and business confidence

I work with many clients who run their own business and, often, they tell me they have great plans but for whatever reason, they cannot get past various obstacles and find themselves procrastinating when it comes to taking themselves to that 'next level'.

A fear of putting yourself out there can be crippling to any business owner, as, in these days of information overload, having your voice heard and being confident in what you offer is essential.

Using EFT, when we dig deeper, we often uncover various fears, which are showing up as inaction, indecision and ultimately an inability to grow and thrive.

Sometimes, EFT can actually uncover a fear of success. No wonder they have been procrastinating!

I worked with an artist, Sarah, who knew she desperately wanted to leave her corporate job and share her art, as this was her real passion, to make a new life for herself in this field.

Fear and doubt had seriously nibbled away at her confidence, and she felt stuck, unable to get out there and be seen. She felt that her work was just not good enough and she could not face the prospect of opening herself up to any negative feedback.

This in turn was keeping her dreams stifled and on hold.

After just one session working together, a few doors of clarity opened for us and we could see that she had *never* been told she was good enough: good enough for anything, let alone being an artist.

Any encouragement she had received had been in the direction of getting good grades. Expressing her individuality or creativity was not a priority in her family, and a lack of praise had left her feeling less than adequate.

EFT enabled her to tap away the anxiety she was experiencing and to see clearly that her concerns about her work were purely her own. The criticism she feared was something she had fabricated. No one had actually said you cannot do it. This was her own inner self-talk holding her back.

After our session, Sarah felt invigorated and willing to face any critics or negativity and just go ahead and do what she wanted to do. This is the ultimate freedom we speak about when we refer to EFT.

Since we worked together, Sarah has been confidently sharing her work with the public and her work has featured at a number of exhibitions. She has truly started out on her journey.

The future

When I think about the future of EFT, I see it very much as a highly effective tool for personal development. I see it giving courage to those who doubt themselves, as it has with me, to help them believe that they can achieve great things and then go on to take the action necessary to make it happen.

I use EFT whenever I have to do something for my business which makes me feel uncomfortable. The incremental benefits of working with the technique make it perfect for helping us to overcome small hurdles, one at a time.

I would not have been able to grow my business without it, as things like writing a blog, sharing on social media, reaching out to new customers and networking would have been too difficult for me before I discovered EFT.

Whenever there is an unhelpful fear holding us back, EFT can help us to see the truth behind that fear and give us the clarity we need to step forward into the best version of ourselves. No more excuses for being a shrinking violet!

EFT: And sports

by Pete Weaver

A soft, dull thud ***echoes*** around the stadium as the ball bounces on the manicured turf. The crowd settles into respectful silence, as if cathedral-like, awaiting a quasi-religious experience. It is match point and he strains to keep his anticipation of victory from bursting through into false reality too soon, as he prepares to serve.

He looks up, finger wiping a bead of sweat from his eyebrow, and sees the number- one seed staring straight back at him, still confident, not yet vanquished. A sudden pang of doubt leaps unbidden into his head.

'Who would I be if I won?' There was a security in being a journeyman pro. There were no expectations; he could make a living from winning a few rounds and then move on to the next tournament. But this was different: this was big. This could change his life. He had never even reached a semi-final before and now being in the final against the number-one seed was suddenly unsettling! Was he ready for this? Perhaps it would not matter if he lost. Everyone expected him to! He would be accepted back into the comfort of the journeyman tribe. He had tweaked his shoulder in the second set and although it did not hurt in the heat of battle, if he thought about it, it was a bit sore and, well, if you are injured that is just bad luck and you are allowed to lose.

'You will never amount to anything, boy' his PE master ***echoes*** from deep in his past.

'You're such a bad boy, you do not deserve anything nice.' His mum agrees from years before.

'Your serve is rubbish. You really have to stop double-faulting if you want to win the under-10 tournament,' his first coach reinforces 6 years later.

Another bounce of the ball, trying to hang on to the ritual that his coach has assured him would maintain his focus and keep him 'in the zone'.

He has hit this serve a thousand times, hard and flat down the middle until biomechanically it is almost perfect. External rotation of the fore-arm, linking to a snap pronation of the wrist sending the ball winging unerringly towards its target at speeds in excess of 120 mph. Twelve times already in the match he has executed this serve to perfection, winning clean aces and leaving his opponent floundering.

But still … The ***ECHO***s (**E**nergetic **C**onscious **H**ol**O**grams) are still flooding into his head or is it his head? It is strange but it feels more like his chest.

'CONCENTRATE!' He chastises himself but it is futile, how can you concentrate on concentrating?

'UNWORTHY' flies through his head from nowhere, unchallenged.

A third bounce. It seems an age since he had moved purposefully to the baseline, slipped the spare ball into his pocket and had decided confidently on the type of serve he would deliver, but in reality it is only a matter of seconds.

'Tennis? Why don't you play rugby like I did? Now that is a real man's game,' his father's voice ***echoes*** from the grave.

'Don't go there!' he pleads, 'not now, of all times!' He recalls the moment he heard that his father had died from a sudden heart attack only hours after they had parted, following yet another heated argument.

His father had never accepted him as a tennis player, never watched him play. Anxious for approval, he had trained hard, harder than anyone else in the squad, driven by a desire to prove something to his father.

Now his proudest moment as a tennis player was here and it was almost as if his father had died on purpose just so he would not have to acknowledge his success. An emotion akin to hate started to rise in his stomach. A sudden wave of guilt immediately countered this. He was horror struck. How could he think such things? And yet there was still an anger that bubbled deep inside that still held on to such thoughts;

but the guilt still hounded him: guilt from thinking such thoughts, guilt that he never had chance to put things right, guilt that perhaps the argument caused his father's death. He knew this was not the first time or the last that these feelings would haunt him. If only there was a way to banish these demons.

A fourth bounce! A panic starts to grow inside. His ritual is three bounces, no tugging of the shirt, no spinning of the racket, just like his coach had taught him, three simple bounces as he visualizes the perfect serve ahead – then do it! But, now, he had bounced it four times and broken his routine, and yet the shock of this departure from his ritual had brought him back to the present and momentarily cleared the internal dialogue from his head. His opponent, sensing nervousness, steps forward one pace, making sure that this threatening movement is noticed! There is a wry smile on his lips. He has been here many times before and recognizes the signs that the maggots are eating away at his opponent's confidence.

In a desperate bid to seize the moment, he tosses the ball into the air and starts to drive his legs up after it. The world stops and the next few moments are played out in slow motion. His shoulders rotate, he drives the butt of the racket up high then cracks the racket head up and out through the ball. The crowd hears the satisfying crack of strings on ball but, to him, it is like a long rumble of thunder. He watches the ball hit the service line, sees the puff of chalk dust explode from the impact, sees the ball crash into the stop netting at the back of the court.

The crowd rises as one, as if through deep water, and his heart leaps in ecstasy as the realization of victory begins to dawn.

But then the unthinkable! Barking across the delirious outpouring of the crowd, he hears the linesman's call, 'OUT!'

His head is numb. His senses whirl in disbelief. A rage starts to build within him almost primeval in its depth. It is out of control, ready to erupt, an emotional volcano of fiery fury. Yet another injustice, the pattern of his life, why is everything so unfair?

Bad line calls, opponent's lucky shots that hit the net and dropped over, the motor- cycle accident and what happened to his girlfriend, riding pillion. It was not his fault! That car just pulled out without looking. It was so unfair. The weight of injustice suddenly feels heavy on his shoulders. His mother not letting him play for his football team on Sundays as it was a day for church, so unfair! No proper part for him in the primary school nativity play. He had so wanted to be Joseph …

'OVERRULE! The ball was good!' The umpire announces within a moment of the initial call. 'First service.'

He feels helpless. It would have been an ace, but he knew the rules – the linesman's call had interrupted play and affected his opponent. But he knew better, that ball was not coming back, call or no call! It was so unfair, don't these guys realise how important their calls are and how they could change a match? Change a life! As much as he wanted to smash his racket into the ground to vent his frustration, he knew that protest was useless. Nothing was going to change. This was just another example of the injustice that he felt had cursed him all his life!

His emotions were in turmoil, yet he knew that he had to drag himself out of this weakened state, the loss of heart, the brittleness of belief. If only there were someone who could help him manage all these feelings, some techniques that could free him from these negative emotions, someway of reimprinting more helpful memories and beliefs!

Well of course those therapists amongst you will know that there is. This pot-pourri of self-destructive emotions, fears and self-limiting beliefs are just some examples of issues that I have dealt with whilst working with athletes from various sports.

Sport is a microcosm of life. It is full of the elation and disappointment, the excitement and frustration, the joy and the pain that life brings.

It mirrors the competitive struggles and the battle for energy that we see in geopolitical situations, boardrooms and personal relationships. The combative sports of boxing, karate and other martial arts are perhaps the most directly confrontational but, despite the emphasis on physicality and technique, the Japanese say that the fight is won or lost in the heart long before it begins.

Similarly, in high-endurance events such as marathon running, whilst immense physical demands are placed on the body, there must be a determination to keep going even when the body is exhausted, or, in other words, you must have the heart to continue.

Other sports rely on more indirect methods of imposing one's energetic strength upon the opponent through a variety of proxies including balls, striking equipment (bats, rackets, sticks, etc.), panels of style judges, and of course the stopwatch. But still we hear commentators use such phrases as 'he is losing heart' or 'she is playing with such belief' and these are the keys that tell us that emotions have such a part to play in sporting performance. The key to success in all these sporting areas is the belief that you can and will win. Where does this belief lie? Well, as usual, our language gives us away: we do not 'believe with all our head', we 'believe with all our heart'. It is a feeling, an emotion, a truth unsubstantiated in our conscious world. In essence, high performance is about doing the right thing, at the right time, in the right place, to the appropriate standard.

In an effort to maximise an athlete's potential, sport science has brought dramatic improvements in all currently identified components of sporting-performance excellence. As a result, there is now a plethora of specialist professionals: physical trainers, bio mechanists, tacticians and sports psychologists but, in my view, there is still an area that has not been covered and that is 'emotional resilience'.

It is in this area that the use of EFT and Matrix Reimprinting can have positive benefits to sporting performance.

So how can we use these powerful techniques to help athletes? There are two main ways, well, three, if we include dealing with the emotional components of sports injury but that is for another day!

Firstly, we must remember that athletes are no different, in an emotional sense, from anyone else. They are subject to the same learned responses, self- limiting beliefs and ***ECHO***s from the past that affect all of us. They can be treated in the same way as any other person. The only slight difference is that instead of using the techniques as a therapy for physical symptoms or 'dis-ease' we are using them to remove blocks to performance. By using standard EFT, we can tap on those negative beliefs and collapse them.

Matrix Reimprinting allows us to work with the athlete tracking back in the Matrix to identify one or more ***ECHOs*** which have created or reinforced those beliefs. By working with those ***ECHOs***, which are trapped in the past, we can go back in time to the occasion when that belief was first imprinted and so resolve it.

The second way we can support athletes is by helping them to 'maintain state'. Every athlete has their own optimum state, which is where they perform at the peak of their ability.

It is largely a subconscious state, which is often characterized by athletes not remembering details of their performance but just a broad recollection of 'being in the zone' or 'feeling the flow' or 'hitting a purple patch'. This is what NLP practitioners would recognize as the 'unconscious competent' stage of the 'accomplished performer'.

The secret of high performance is to be able to access this state as often as possible. In Matrix Reimprinting we access ***ECHO***s that have split off as a result of the freeze response. In times of stress adrenaline, cortisol and norepinephrine are released and the biochemistry of the body changes to prepare it for intense physical muscular activity.

In a similar way, the body chemistry changes in times of great joy or ecstasy. There is a range of hormones associated with the state of happiness: serotonin, oxytocin, endorphins, dopamine, phenylethylamine and ghrelin and each of these has an effect on the body's chemistry when released.

Visualisation is a technique used by athletes to rehearse performance, in an effort to allow the subconscious mind to replicate high performance in the future.

By entering the Matrix with our athlete, we can search out examples of good ***ECHO***s, where high-quality performance has been achieved before. I call these good ***ECHO***s – '***GECHO***s' and use the gecko illustration to visually represent them. (see Figure 1)

As it happens, the gecko symbolizes power, mobility, agility and flexibility, so it is particularly appropriate to most athletes.

(Figure 1)

By working with these '***GECHO***s,' using the Matrix protocols, we can build up a vivid picture for the athlete to step into and immerse themselves in the energy of success. We can then use NLP anchoring techniques to allow the athlete to access this energy at the appropriate time, either in preparation for a match or to regain state during the contest.

EFT: For financial healing

by Mark Bristow

My journey to EFT

And as Karl Dawson finished the point he was making, it felt like the final piece of the jigsaw had fallen into place. At that moment, I also realized, not for the first time, I had been searching in the wrong place! Even more frustrating was the fact that it was not even the first time I had attended a Matrix Reimprinting course. I was actually assisting on this one. Finally, to cap it all, this topic had also been covered in my NLP (Neuro Linguistic Programming) training.

The feeling of frustration was soon tapped away and I was left knowing I was now in a position where I could share my knowledge with the world, or at least with those who wanted to listen!

Until that moment, I had spent most of my life as a human 'doing' rather than a human 'being'. Despite everything appearing great at a conscious level, a loving family, lots of friends and a steady job, something was missing.

The first clue as to why I acted the way I did came during a short exercise in my NLP training when I realized the authentic me had no need for recognition. At the time, the level of income from my day job was dependent upon how much money I brought into the company. I was working in an environment where recognition and money were closely associated and yet I got the biggest buzz from helping people who found themselves in financial trouble, rather than adding a few noughts onto clients' net worth. For me, it was about the helping, not the money.

So, I quit my job and set out to help as many people as I could. I missed my work colleagues but, overnight, my stress levels dropped dramatically. However, it was not until that fateful day with Karl that everything fell into place.

So what was it Karl said that made the change?

Quite simply, how we act on a day-to-day basis is driven by our beliefs. Henry Ford once famously said, 'whether you think you can, or whether you think you cannot, you are right.' Those of you familiar with the work of Bruce Lipton will know core beliefs are created at a very young age and are held in our subconscious. They may be so deep in our subconscious that we may not even be aware of them at a conscious level and, as they are created at such a young age, they are probably no longer relevant in adult life.

So how does this fit specifically into EFT and money?

You and I know that in order to have money, we need to spend less than we earn. Why is it then that so many people fail to stick to that very basic principle? On the outside, they have houses full of the latest furniture and gadgets, buy designer clothes and run expensive cars but are maxed out on numerous credit and store cards in order to live this lifestyle. Why do so many of my clients have no problem making money but are unable to keep hold of it?

In order to create the relationship we want with money, we have to seek out the underlying reasons why we spend more than we earn, or, seemingly, why we are not able to keep hold of what we have. We do this at a subconscious level.

Of all the issues that I have dealt with, I think that this is the one where our parents and their own beliefs have the most influence.

So if you can remember being told 'money doesn't grow on trees' or 'we are not made of money', it is it likely these beliefs buried themselves in you and are held in your subconscious. If you hold these beliefs, is it any wonder you have a poor relationship with money? You may not believe these expressions are true at a conscious level but, held in your subconscious, they form your belief. Even if you believe an expression to be true, such as 'money can't buy you happiness', it can have a negative implication. For example, money is not a good thing as it cannot buy you happiness.

Fortunately, we have the tools available to get deep into our subconscious. I wanted to combine some of the best bits of NLP and EFT to complement each other. In my one-to-one work with clients, I prefer to use Matrix Reimprinting rather than EFT scripts as Matrix offers more freedom to go wherever seems right with a particular issue. However, I am a strong believer in the power of momentum and clients working on themselves in between sessions. With this is mind, I developed what I call Outcome Based EFT.

Outcome Based EFT

First, you need to identify the negative belief (the issue) and the desired outcome. So for example, the negative belief may be 'I am no good with money'.

Next, determine whether this belief is actually true. What evidence is there to support it? Could the opposite be true? What evidence can you think of that supports this opposite viewpoint?

If answering these questions does not cause a shift, you need to consider what is your desired outcome. For this, you need to ask:

What would be preferable to believing that 'I am no good with money'?

While the obvious answer would seem to be 'I am good with money', I have noticed that, with my clients, this is rarely the case. It may be something like 'I want the security of knowing there will always be enough money for me to live my authentic life'.

Finally, in order to focus on your outcome, you need to ask yourself when you want it. If the answer is anything other than now, you may want to ask yourself why.

Having determined your issue and your outcome, the next step is to tune into your emotions. When you think about your negative belief around money and wealth, which emotion does this evoke? Where in your body do you feel this? Describe how this emotion feels and looks, the size, texture, whether it has a colour, etc.

Now ask yourself if there is any good reason to hold on to this belief. This may need some consideration rather than to opt for the seemingly obvious answer as, often under the surface, there can lie perceived secondary gains by holding on to the belief. You may then wish to ask yourself what would be the consequences of letting go of this belief.

To recap, here is the process:

- Identify your negative beliefs about money.
- Which is the most prominent belief?
- Is this negative belief true? What evidence is there to support this?
- Could the opposite be true? Is there evidence to suggest that the opposite is true?
- What would be more preferable than your current belief? (Avoid stating the opposite.)
- When do you want this outcome?
- When you tune in to this belief, how does it make you feel, and where? What size and weight is it? Does it have a colour?
- What is the emotion you associate with this feeling?
- Is there any good reason to hold on to this negative belief?
- If this process has not provided a big enough shift, it is time to tap.

Outcome EFT tapping procedure

I should point out here that I use the tapping points as taught by Karl Dawson. (see Diagram 2)

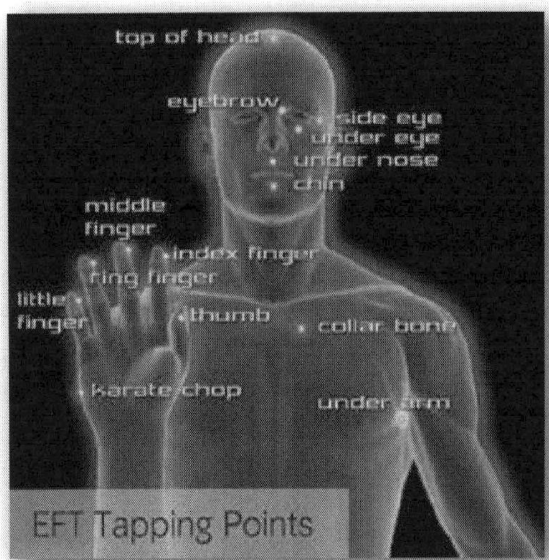

(Diagram 2)

These are not in any way cast in stone and I would recommend that you adapt the script to suit your own tapping style. I have also included a set-up statement, which you may choose to exclude.

Let us use the previous example of 'I am no good with money' and assume the emotion is frustration, which manifests as a brown sharp pain in the solar plexus.

Set up Statement

Karate Chop Point (KC). "Even though I am no good with money, I completely love and accept myself."

KC: "Even though I have this frustrated brown, sharp pain in my solar plexus, I completely love and accept myself."

KC: "Even though I have this brown, sharp pain of frustration in my solar plexus because I am no good with money, I completely love and accept myself."

Top of Head (TH) "I am no good with money"

Eye Brow (EB) "All this frustration"

Outside Eye (OE) "This brown sharp pain of frustration"

Under Eye (UE) "This brown sharp pain in my solar plexus"

Under Nose (UN) "This frustration in my solar plexus"

Under Lower Lip (UL) "I let go of this frustration"

Collar Bone (CB) "I let go of the knot"

Under Arm (UA) "There will always be enough money for me"

Thumb (THB) "I have proof of that"

Index Finger (IF) "I have enough money to be secure"

Middle Finger (MF) “I choose to have enough money”

Ring Finger (RF) “I love to have enough money”

Little Finger (LF) “I can be my authentic self”

A few rounds of tapping should see a shift but, unfortunately, this is not normally the end of the story.

While Outcome Based EFT can be used to help remove negative beliefs around money, we have only removed a few layers of the onion. We need to get to the core belief and can do this by asking some supplementary questions.

Say, for example, the perceived issue is that ‘I can make money but I can’t keep hold of it’, you simply ask yourself:

‘And how does that make me feel?’

The answer may be:

‘Well I feel that, at my age, I should be able to keep hold of money.’

Again, ask:

‘And how does that make me feel?’

'Well it makes me feel that I am a bit stupid.'

Again:

'How does that make me feel?'

'It makes me feel that I am not good enough.'

Now you have arrived at our core issue, you can ask the Outcome Based EFT questions:

1. 'What is my current issue?'
   'The negative belief I have about myself.'
2. 'What is the most prominent belief?'
   'I am not good enough.'
3. 'Is this negative belief true? What evidence is there to support this?'
   'At work, colleagues with less knowledge and worse people skills were more successful than me.'
4. 'Could the opposite be true? Is there evidence to suggest that the opposite is true?'
   'I was successful against a large number of candidates in securing a recruitment position in one of the UK's largest life assurance companies.'
5. 'What would be more preferable than your current belief?' (Avoid stating the opposite.)
   'Feeling happy in my own skin.'

6. 'When you tune in to this belief, how does it make you feel inside, and where? What size and weight is it? Does it have a colour?'
   'Like a dark weight on my shoulders.'
7. 'Which emotion do you associate with this feeling?'
   'Sadness – that I have lived like this for so long.'
8. 'When do you want this outcome?'
   'Now.'
9. 'Is there any good reason to hold on to this negative belief?'
   'No.'

Start the tapping process with the Set up Statement:

KC: "Even though, I feel that I am not good enough, I completely love and accept myself"

KC: "Even though I have this dark weight on my shoulders, I completely love and accept myself"

KC: "Even though I have this dark weight of sadness on my shoulders, I completely love and accept myself"

TH: "I am not good enough"

EB: "I am not good enough"

OE: "All this sadness"

UE: "This weight on my shoulders"

UN: "This sadness in my shoulders"

UL: "I let go of this weight"

CB: "I let go of this dark weight"

UA: "I am good enough"

THB: "I have proof that I am good enough"

IF: "I want to be happy in my own skin"

MF: "I choose to be happy in my own skin"

RF: "I love to be happy in my own skin"

LF: "I am happy in my own skin"

As one client said, "Ah, I get it now. This is really about self-worth and not net worth. Our financial situation is a reflection of how we feel about ourselves. I guess this reflection shows up in other areas such as health, relationships and in our careers."

The two-step process, outlined here, is recommended for those who are new to EFT or feel that easing in to the core issue is preferable. It is possible to ask the further questions straight away and get straight to the core issue.

The Outcome Based EFT process clarifies the starting and end points which enable you to be specific and, as Gary Craig says, 'Be specific to be terrific!'

If this tapping process brings up memories that are too traumatic for you to deal with on your own, I strongly suggest that you work with a fully qualified EFT / Matrix Reimprinting practitioner.

Once the core issue has been identified, it is possible for change to happen quite quickly. For me, I experienced a gradual change as I learned to love myself more. I focused on enjoying the journey and would often look back to check how far I had come.

From having a limited belief that I would spend all my life working in the same industry, I soon found I had almost too many ideas about which direction I should take. In the end, I left it to the universe to decide. As a result, I carried on Erik Cornish's concept of 'The Financial Healer' and wrote the book of the same name.

The future

I am hoping that *The Financial Healer* book will be my legacy and my way of getting the message of EFT, NLP and Matrix Reimprinting out to a larger audience.

And as for money not buying happiness. It does not, but try living without it.

Seriously, it is not how much money you have, it is what it will give you. Will it give you peace of mind if you can meet all your living expenses and have some left over? Yes, it most probably will. Will it buy you happiness? Probably not.

Ultimately, I believe it is about having enough money to live your authentic lifestyle. If more money comes into your life, you can use it to help others, and what a great feeling it is when you can!

So when are you going to change your self- worth to increase your net worth?

EFT: For long-term health conditions

by Sharon Branagh

My journey to EFT

Only medication will work. Well, that is what I was told the day I was diagnosed with a long-term health condition, an incurable chronic disease. I could not believe it. At first, I felt relieved because at least I knew there was a reason why I was feeling so ill with pain everywhere, an all over flu-like feeling; foggy head, no energy, even getting out of bed drained me. And then, I got annoyed. Why has this happened to me? I was normally really healthy and no one in my family had had this so it could not have been genetic.

I put my faith in the medical professionals (because they know best, right?) and did what I was told by trying all the medications I was offered. None stopped the symptoms and some made me feel worse. I gained weight, lost hair and generally deteriorated. At one stage, I found it difficult to walk. I asked the medical professionals again, 'what can I do to help myself? Should I change my diet or try alternative treatments?' I was willing to try anything. But I got the same answer: 'Only medication will work, let's try the next one until we find one that works for you'. I just did not believe that only medication would work and deep down, I knew that there was something else I could do to help myself. So, with an open mind, I started to try other things.

I went for acupuncture (I hated needles so that was a big deal for me!) and found that, for some reason, it helped. I was intrigued to learn how poking needles in to the skin could help me feel better. I researched meridian theory and that is how I came across EFT Tapping and the start of my health-changing journey. I learnt that the body has an energy system, something that, despite all my training in behaviour analysis and psychotherapeutic interventions, I had not been taught before. I learnt that by tapping and talking, I could literally reduce pain, resolve difficult emotions, deal with difficult memories from my past and resolve limiting/negative beliefs. Wow!

So why do chronic diseases and long-term conditions happen in the first place? Approximately 5 to 6 per cent of the world's population are born with a genetic disorder and our DNA is only switched on or off in response to what is affecting it within its environment. So what else could cause them? I asked the medical professionals and it turns out that the causes of most diseases are 'unknown'. There is increasing evidence to suggest a huge contributory factor is stress and I agree, the word itself is telling us what is wrong – it is in 'dis-ease'.

What I have also learnt along the way is that the body is not actually against you. It is serving to protect you and is only adapting and responding to the mental and emotional states that it has been under. We know the mind and body are connected through a biofeedback loop of information, which goes back and forth.

There are millions of neurotransmitters (brain messengers) and the neuropathways in your brain can actually change by thinking differently, through a process called neuroplasticity. You think something, which makes you feel a certain way, which then affects your behaviour or how you react and this can make you think, feel and behave differently (and so on). For example, when we think something positive, we tend to feel positive and do something positive. Likewise, negative thoughts can make us feel negative and this affects our behaviour.

It makes sense that the body responds to what the mind has been thinking and vice versa.

Continuous 'dis-ease' in the mind is therefore bound to cause 'dis-ease' in the body.

Emotional stress causes many physical symptoms and is a major contributor to pain.

In fact, around 80 per cent of all psychotherapeutic interventions address the emotional aspect of an issue. But what are emotions? Well they are just 'energy in motion' but to make sense of them, we tend to give them labels. For example, we might feel some energy in our stomach, a butterflies feeling and we might label this as anxiety if we are waiting to go into an exam, or excitement if we receive a gift. It is the same energy but we call it something different depending on the situation around us. So what if we recognized and accepted the emotion (energy) without resisting it?

Emotions, like thoughts, come and go all the time, so, if we allowed them to, they would flow without getting stuck or blocked. However, let us say someone has stressful thoughts and in turn resists or holds onto their emotions. The brain releases the necessary electromagnetic signals, chemicals, proteins and energy via the autonomic nervous system to the body so it can cope with that message. Now, these messages could be in response to a real threat, danger or trauma that is happening in the here and now or it could be in response to something imagined, like stressful thoughts. The mind does not know the difference between reality and imagination and either way, the body will do what it needs in order to protect itself. Now, the good thing about the fight-or-flight response is that the body gets to discharge the energy connected to that specific event, because you run or fight back.

However, with the freeze response (often triggered in trauma), the energy just gets trapped or stuck inside the body. If the body is 'holding on' physically (because it does not want to let go) and if this message is given enough times to the body, guess what 'dis-ease' might happen? Constipation – the body could become constipated. This was certainly true for a 44-year-old female who was a case study of mine.

From a very young age she always had to keep her emotions in. She was not allowed to let herself go or to be herself. She experienced childhood situations where that message was reinforced so she started to see proof in that belief and, as a result, found that she was always tense, uptight and unable to fully relax and let go. Fast forward 40 years and she now has a diagnosis of chronic constipation. For her, tapping literally helped her allow the energy that was stuck to move freely and as she started to resolve emotional issues, the physical issues resolved themselves too.

Being diagnosed with a long-term health condition or chronic disease can be life changing. It can be difficult to come to terms with, practically, physically and emotionally. There are many difficulties that you have to deal with and it is easy to get caught up in a negative perpetuating cycle, where you cannot see the wood for the trees or the light at the end of the tunnel.

The more you think of something, the more you will feel it. For example, the more I focused on pain, the more pain I felt. It can be so difficult to see anything else beyond what you feel in that moment. Over time, the condition might even start to have some benefits.

Case study

Let me give you examples of people I have worked with. One woman suffered chronic migraines to the point where they caused her to be bed bound for almost a week. She literally had to shut herself away in the dark and keep everyone out until she got over them. I asked her, 'How could this condition be serving or protecting you?' After becoming slightly shocked at the idea that this condition might serve a purpose, she actually considered the benefits. She was able to shut herself away from all the stress of work, she stopped running around after her mother and, for a week, people didn't expect her to do anything. She was allowed to be by herself and shut out the world.

Another example is a retired horse-groom who developed generalized anxiety disorder following a riding accident. She found that, since her accident, and, after being diagnosed, her children came to her house to see her, she was not expected to look after her grandchildren all the time and she got more attention from her husband. When I asked if she was ready to let go of the anxiety, there was a part of her that did not want to return to the life of being 'put on' by her children and she was afraid she might lose the attention that she was getting from her husband.

These examples show that subconsciously a long-term health condition can serve a fundamental purpose and at times the secondary gains might keep it going.

So if you have or know anyone who has a health condition, think about what the body is doing and consider what it might be telling you.

For example, one of my very first EFT case studies was with a man who had a slipped disc. I asked what it felt like to experience this pain and he said it felt like a right pain in the bum! I asked him who or what situation in his life has been a right pain in the bum.

He started laughing because he was having issues with one of his children. You could also ask the questions:

- How might the condition be serving you?
- What might having this condition stop you from doing?
- How can this be protecting you in some way?
- Is there any reason to hold onto this condition?
- What would change if you got better?

I have found that addressing these underlying issues is a fundamental starting point to returning to health following a long-term condition. A tree has leaves, branches, a trunk and roots. Using the 'EFT Tapping Tree' is a symbolic, effective and systematic way to address the symptoms (pain), emotions (frustrations), significant events (distressing memories) and limiting beliefs (e.g. thinking you will never get better), connected with a chronic disease or a long-term health condition.

Now, I am no tree surgeon but even I know that if you pulled out all of the roots of a tree then the tree would find it hard to exist! So, using EFT on limiting beliefs can be effective for getting down to core issues and, just like the domino effect, it will change the events, emotions and symptoms associated with the condition. I have given clients the tapping tree diagram created by Lindsay Kenny and used in The *Tapping Solution for Pain Relief* by Nick Ortner so they can list their symptoms, emotions, events and limiting beliefs connected to their condition as a way to focus on what to tap on.

On very bad days, I used to combine Slow/Positive and Energy EFT. I would tap through the points very slowly and using deep breaths either side of saying the thing that I wanted. For me, when I was really poorly, I needed energy. I used this as a pro-active and reactive strategy, so for 10 minutes every morning I would tap and sometimes, throughout the day if I needed a top-up of more energy. I started at the top of the head, tapping then taking a breath and saying 'energy', then another breath and tapping some more, before moving onto the next point.

When using standard EFT on symptom management, I found adjusting the set-up statement beneficial. For example, when I was in excruciating pain, I did not feel as though I 'deeply and completely love[d] and accept[d] myself anyway'. Some days, the only thing I felt like saying was 'at least I am doing something about it anyway'. Because of my experience with this, I encouraged my clients to finish their set-up statements using something that they actually believed about themselves or their situation in that moment, rather than using the typical set-up statement.

I found that people felt more authentic with what they were saying and they had faster and more effective results. So, if you wanted to use EFT on a symptom like pain, your set-up statement could be something like 'even though, I have this pain, I am doing something about it anyway'. You would then get more specific by describing the pain, the shape, colour, density, and so on. I always finish a round of EFT tapping by holding the wrist and taking a deep breath. This not only gives a good opportunity to check back in with the pain levels and monitor progress, but it also encourages oxygen to the brain and body, especially if you use diaphragmatic breathing (known as belly breathing).

The future

There are increasingly more published studies which show the efficacy of EFT for the treatment of long-term conditions. In fact, a recent scientific study evidenced that on average, after just 20 minutes of tapping, participants' pain levels dropped by 68 per cent! I am encouraged to find the NHS are now commissioning MBSR (mindfulness based stress reduction) and other self-management courses, which are helping people return to health, and I envisage that, before long, other complementary therapies, such as EFT, will be freely available on the NHS. The clinical trials and data just need to keep proving its effectiveness. Personally, it has helped me and I have witnessed transformations in the lives of those who I have worked with.

Along with EFT I would always advocate a holistic approach to health which includes:

- working with your healthcare professional;
- taking medication as prescribed;
- drinking quality water;
- getting adequate rest (including a meditation practice);
- pacing yourself;
- taking appropriate exercise (including something that uses the mind, body and spirit, like tai chi or yoga);
- healthy eating (seven fruit or vegetables a day and cutting out processed foods);
- getting restful sleep;
- avoidance of alcohol/drugs or other stimulants and toxins;
- getting adequate sunlight;
- reducing stress.

So, other things (along with medication) do work!

EFT: And horses

by Emma Bailey

My journey to EFT

Reflections from the horse

Like many little girls, I always loved ponies, always enjoyed donkey rides on the beach, trekking on holidays and riding lessons growing up. There is something exhilarating and slightly scary about sitting on half a ton of horse and I was not always that confident but I was never-endingly curious.

My passion for these wonderful creatures steadily grew through adulthood until I was taking professional exams, schooling horses and escorting rides out. I found horses gave me a new confidence in myself, a new passion for life, and a new sense that I would never be alone. It had dawned on me that 'horse' was an international language; you could go anywhere in the world and ride a horse, meet new people and make new friends.

It was a chance encounter with a woman rescuing horses in Turkey during 1997 which really changed my perspective and my journey. Through her, I learned of classical equitation and the world of nurturing abused and neglected horses; but it was a rescued mare named Brandy who led me to see myself in a whole new perspective, to learning energy healing and making a promise 'to do whatever I could, whenever I could, for the welfare of horses'.

One day when walking Brandy in from the field, my heart was consumed by how anyone could have mistreated such a beautiful horse so badly. With these thoughts in my head as I looked at her, I saw her looking back at me in the same way. I suddenly had this deep realisation that she did not define me by labels. She just saw my soul, saw me for who I was in that moment in time. The power of connection in that moment changed me. It shifted my whole perspective and started my journey into now.

I believe that we are not defined by the labels others place on us or the labels we place on others.

It is powerful to realize that you are not just the girl with the cleft lip and palate. You are not worthless or lesser than anyone else. You are you in your heart and the only thing that is limiting you is your acceptance of self. The horse accepts and responds to you totally as who you are in that moment. They see your conflicts and your fears and bring them to the surface of your being. What a gift that beautiful horse gave me and continues to give me every day. She sits deep inside my heart, connecting me to source, guiding me from afar, and yet still so near. My love for her is not diminished but, rather, strengthened by time and space.

As a consequence, I not only continued to explore classical horsemanship and horse behaviour, including positive training methods, but I went on with my own healing journey. Although my journey started with Reiki, I went on to learn Neuro Linguistic Programming, Hypnotherapy, Time Line Therapy™, before finally discovering the wonderful world of EFT.

EFT affords the most wonderfully gentle mechanisms for bringing people and horses together, to resolve issues, deepen bonds, to nurture self-acceptance, and it has been my great privilege to explore this work.

Case studies

Reflections in perspective

Horses have so much to offer us in terms of learning and reflection. So often, how they respond to people can reflect what is going on in that person's life. Just as Brandy had changed my life, my desire and purpose to help people and horses grew too.

I worked with a lovely woman and her mare some years ago. The mare was seen to be very 'dominant' and with a mind of her own. Consequently, the woman had become nervous of riding her. We started one session with some work from the ground and as I watched, the woman was working a lot harder than the horse! I asked her what she thought was going on and she replied, 'She's walking all over me.' We decided to use EFT to tap directly on this thought: 'Even though she's walking all over me, I love her and me anyway.'

It is wonderful to watch the dynamic of energy shift through even one simple round of tapping, as the horse started to move out of her owner's space and to walk around her gently. Further rounds of EFT led to the mare being completely focused on her owner's body language and energy and I witnessed a beautiful harmony and connection between the two. This ability of the horse to be flexible always and to stay in the 'present' is a salutary lesson to be absorbed and cherished.

As humans, we often learn to bury our self-expression; that we should not say this or should not feel that. It is this suppression of who we really are that causes stress and anxiety. Horses not only have stronger energy fields than us, five times that of a human, they also help to bring us into the present, into a place of being, where all our fears can be laid bare, acknowledged and tapped upon.

This particular client had several EFT sessions allowing her to resolve and release past bullying issues and personal insecurities. Her clever mare reflected the shifts in her every step of the way and provided a valuable and delightful feedback mechanism for change.

Be the calm in the storm

What I love about EFT is that it rebalances the energy for the horse as well as the handler.

Some horses have been key in my learning, not least a horse named Jimmy, an ex-racehorse who had been in five racing yards and then had three private owners by the time he was eight.

I often think of the parallels with troubled foster children in these situations. For many of us just moving school or home with our family can be a daunting prospect but to be shunted around never knowing where you will end up next must be overwhelming at times and no doubt underlie many behavioural problems, especially as trust must be hard to maintain.

Jimmy was one such case where his behaviour had been extremely affected by his experiences. He distrusted people and took no comfort or security from them and his default position was to react in the extreme to anything that bothered him, frequently standing on his hind legs or biting and nipping. Having come into contact and used EFT with some abused and consequently fostered children, I realised the parallels were great; not least the anger constantly bubbling to the surface and spilling over– probably the only survival tool in the armoury that kept them going when life was just too much to handle.

How wonderful, therefore, to have a tool like EFT which can so gently and easily release trauma and childhood issues, allowing that anger to be released and giving a way forward for so many.

EFT certainly helped to start Jimmy on the road to being more at peace with humans, not to overreact to everything, not to feel so traumatized and finally to start trusting that there were some people that he could rely on to look after him with kindness. I worked a lot on his inner- child issues not least around the trauma of the loss of his mother, which, I felt, he blamed people for and was at the root of much of his anger and anxiety.

I always loved how demonstrative he was when we were doing EFT, telling you exactly what was going on emotionally or physically for him and I thank him for all the lessons I learned from him – about being present and observing what was happening in the moment.

One of the greatest challenges and biggest lessons, however, was learning to control my own energy around him. When a horse is emotionally explosive, you can feel your heart almost ricocheting with the vibration. As a healing practitioner or therapist of any kind, one of the greatest gifts you can give your client is to 'be the calm in the storm', not to let yourself get swept away by the tides of emotion. I continually work with horses for my own reflective practice, and I offer this service to other therapists too. Horses bring out the subtle nuances of your own energy, which may sit outside of awareness.

Another key point I have learned over the years is that EFT works much better with the horse loose in the field so he or she has a choice as to how near they want to be to you, so they do not feel restricted or controlled. Time and again, I have found that a more organic, 'go-with-the-flow', 'treat-the-herd' type tapping results in more profound effects in balancing the equilibrium. Horses do not operate in isolation. They understand the being of oneness that we humans so often aspire to. Working with them in this way gives far better feedback, flow and truth to the work.

From here to now

Over the years, my journey has afforded me the joy of meeting many wonderful and inspirational people, as well as horses, who have given so generously of their love and time.

I have also witnessed great shifts in the sands of time, as now a vast number of horse owners have used animal communicators and many have heard of Tapping. Minds are opening and becoming more receptive, as science equally is expanding in its knowledge of the heart and energy fields. New theories abound and growing evidence is starting to support the ancient shamanic beliefs underpinning much of today's energy work.

The future

I'LL DO WHAT I CAN, WHENEVER I CAN, FOR THE WELFARE OF HORSES

Over the years, my own use of EFT too has evolved, shifted and grown. Horses provide such invaluable reflections and insights and, more latterly, I have expanded my work to include more mindful-based meridian therapies, such as Inner RePatterning, which I have also developed to be used whilst riding.

The results of this work excite and uplift me as I see profound changes occurring, especially in the depth of relaxation and connection that can be achieved between horse and owner, as tension and old limitations are released. As time goes on, I am exploring, growing and expanding this area of practice, as I believe our own journey can be enhanced so much by reflecting on the lessons from nature.

Mostly, I wish to share with people how to kick up their hooves in the mud a little more and allow their manes to fly in the wind with the sheer joy of life!

Wishing you a joyfully peaceful journey x

EFT: Fears, phobias and academic research

by Dr. Elizabeth Boath

My journey to EFT

A massive spider and a professor in public health introduced me to EFT. Yes, you read that correctly … all will be revealed. It was an incredibly stressful period of my life. (Young twins, full-time job, studying part-time, running a home and generally spinning work plates and juggling family life at the same time.) Until finally the stress of keeping so many balls in the air hit home.

In my quest to get myself into a more balanced life, a friend lent me Roger Callahan's seminal book *Tapping the Healer within*. As an academic psychologist, I was interested, but my rational brain kept saying 'tapping acupressure points, voicing feelings in my body, following algorithms … do not be ridiculous, Liz'. However, a curious little voice kept saying: 'Well if I was a lunatic or Charlatan, aiming to establish a new therapy … I would be developing something far more acceptable than this weird tapping thingy … so perhaps there is something in this.'

Then, home alone one day with my twins, the spider showed up half-way up the stairs. It was enormous, hairy and clearly planning to leap at me as soon as I got anywhere near. Trapped upstairs by this terrifying, hirsute arachnid and realizing that I needed to get downstairs to discover the mischief my now worryingly quiet children were up to, I made a few vain attempts to dash past. Then, I spotted the weird 'tapping' book. Quickly, I grabbed it, flicked to the section on phobias and, book in one hand, I started tapping with the other. Of course, it was not going to work. However, after a few rounds of my very novice tapping, I realised I wasn't quite as fearful and took a step forward with each round, until after about 5 minutes, I realised that, the closer I stepped towards that spider, the smaller and less scarily hairy the spider actually got. A few more rounds and I was finally able to walk (yes, walk) past the now rather small innocuous-looking spider. Fuelled by my success in overcoming my arachnophobia, I mentioned my experience to a colleague, Professor Tony Stewart, who, it turned out, had recently trained in EFT and was interested in doing some research on it. Within a month, I had booked onto an EFT training course and my path to becoming an emotional freedom fighter had begun.

As an academic psychologist, I was keen to explore the research and evidence base for EFT and was surprised to find that there actually was a growing body of research on EFT. Enthused, I started gathering all the research evidence I could find and, subsequently, wrote a systematic review of it with Tony. The next step was to carry out my own research.

Case studies

I had noticed that many of my students suffered from presentation anxiety, particularly around assessments, and so I managed to secure a research grant to carry out a small pilot study, using EFT to reduce anxiety in students. Low and behold it worked! However, this was with complementary therapy students who were very accepting of complementary approaches and who were mainly older women seeking a second career. So, I decided to replicate the research with a more traditional, younger, male-dominated cohort. Although they were initially a lot more sceptical about EFT, much to their surprise – and mine – their anxiety levels also reduced and in a follow-up focus group, many of those sceptical sports science students reported using EFT in their everyday life as well as to enhance their sporting performance. Over the last 3 years, Tony and I have published six EFT research papers and carried out three systematic reviews of EFT research.

For the last 25 years, I have had a strong interest in perinatal mental health and have a PhD in this field, so it made perfect sense for me to combine this with EFT. I do not currently run a private practice. I am way too busy being a mum, an associate professor in health and co- chairing the Association for the Advancement of Meridian Energy Therapies (AAMET) Research Committee, including arranging the first ever UK EFT Scientific Symposium at Staffordshire University. I am, however, often asked to 'do some EFT' with friends, relatives and colleagues.

One woman springs to mind. Tokophobia is a morbid fear of pregnancy and childbirth, and one friend asked for some EFT on the suggestion of her midwife and obstetrician, who had come to the end of their list of traditional, tried and tested medical methods. She was eight months pregnant with her first child and her obstetrician had agreed reluctantly to a planned Caesarean, as her anxiety levels were so high and she was so terrified of childbirth. She was keen to try tapping, though, to keep her calm through her elective Caesarean. I introduced her to tapping and as her anxiety abated, she began asking how she might use it during the birth. I suggested that she show her husband how to tap and that he could tap on her if she wanted; and also that she alert the clinical and ward staff, so that they would know what 'this weird tapping thing' was that she was doing. She began to ask how she might use tapping during a 'normal delivery'. I gave her some suggestions and as she tapped, we talked through different ideas. As the session progressed, she started to wonder whether she might be able to go for a 'normal delivery' after all.

I suggested some 'own work' for her to do and we arranged another session a week later. However, the baby had other plans. She said she had been tapping meticulously each day for 3 days and that her husband was tapping along with her. On the fourth day, her waters broke and she used EFT to stay calm and relaxed during the first stage of labour and was then able to choose to go ahead with a vaginal delivery – with the security blanket of the Caesarean option on standby.

She did not need it. A few days later, she texted to say that she was thrilled and that she was now using EFT to deal with the fun and games of being a new mum.

The future

I love carrying out EFT research and the overwhelming message from EFT research to date is that EFT works. However, there is still a need for a large-scale randomised controlled trial and I will continue on my quest to obtain funding for what is deemed to be the gold standard in health research. I believe that, as the evidence base for EFT continues to grow and the quality of the published research grows too, more and more systematic reviews will be published and that we will soon reach the tipping point of Tapping where it will become harder and harder for EFT to be kept out of the mainstream. When that day arrives, as EFT is so quick to teach and easy to use, it may also become part of the solution to the ever-growing demands on the health service. Indeed, that day is not too far off and this is reflected in the shift in research focus, where the more burning question has shifted from 'Does EFT work?' to 'How does EFT work?' I for one cannot wait to find out.

EFT: And building ultimate confidence

by Tania A. Prince

My journey to EFT

In my EFT private practice, I specialise in working with confidence issues. It is an area that I am very passionate about. I love seeing people reach their full potential. EFT has been a great tool that has helped me transform people's lives countless times. I also believe that, if we train people in EFT, which I do, we have to have ultimate confidence.

The impact of shyness on my early life

Being confident is something I have always aspired to from a young age. I admired confident people because they were the complete opposite of me. I had all of the typical behaviours that go with shyness. I could not speak up in a group and I could not ask questions in class. The underlying reason for this was that I was too frightened of getting things wrong and being told off or ridiculed for this. So, like many shy people, I protected myself by holding back, not speaking up. But this came at a cost. Making yourself invisible, which was what this effectively did for me, might protect you, but it also hinders you in other ways. I got left out. If there were four chairs in the classroom, I would stand back, let the most confident children grab them and then be left standing there feeling awkward and uncomfortable.

No friends, the lonely years

This shyness resulted in me being friendless by the time I reached my teenage years. I spent endless hours in the school playground by myself, not a friend in sight. Luckily, I came from a big family and I was totally confident interacting with my siblings. As a result of this, I often refused to go to school. My mother gave in to me, letting me stay off whenever I wanted. I did, however, love learning. In the time I was off school, I studied. I had a passion for knowledge, which resulted in me doing well academically.

Building my confidence

When I started college, I was able to make friends. By the time I went to university, I had turned this around naturally, to some degree. I had lots of close friends. My confident side certainly came to the forefront. That is the interesting thing about shyness. You can have an extremely confident part of you and a shyness program existing side by side in the same person. My true self was the confident natural person and that is why, from such a young age, I knew I needed to remove this shyness limitation on myself.

I left university and, within a year, went into show business. Again, I put this down to truly wanting to free myself of the limitations I had acquired in my early life. However, the limitations affected my success. For one thing, I should have moved to London but I did not. I held back in fully pushing our act for the fear of rejection and criticism. These fears are a common part of a lack of confidence and shyness. Even with these limitations, I performed in my dance act, which

I co-choreographed with my sister. I formed and managed a rock band and I even acted on TV. My lack of confidence was only obviously evident during radio or TV interviews and acting.

The impact of EFT

EFT is a fabulous tool when it comes to releasing the limitations that hold us back in life. EFT helped me clear my lack of confidence completely. I no longer have an issue giving interviews. I feel free to be myself.

After clearing the problem completely, you realise just how many areas of your life it was affecting. For example, I am no longer thinking in my head, 'what should I say?', 'what will people think if I say that?' These are the more subtle ways a problem like this impacts on you. As a consequence, I find it much easier to converse with people. If you are thinking in your head what to say, you often miss the opportunity, as the conversation moves on.

Using the knowledge I gained from my shyness

As a consequence of my early life experiences, I found myself drawn to helping people discover and free their confident self. This led to me doing a lot of work with those who fear public speaking and have confidence issues. I must admit this is a particular area I love working in. It gives me immense pleasure to help people free themselves from their limitations and discover their true confident self. My experiences with this problem are invaluable as many people think that their problems are unique to them, which they are not. You repeatedly see the same patterns occurring with this problem.

Case studies

Scary teacher case

One client, who came to my clinic years ago, had to present as part of his job. The fact that he felt so nervous doing this was holding him back. He wanted to progress in his career. However, being able to do this requires the ability to present yourself in a confident manner. This problem was holding him back. I used EFT with this client.

One of the interesting things you can do with EFT is use it to uncover the event or events in the client's life that could be the cause of their current problem. Once this is discovered, you can then tap using EFT until the event from their past no longer affects them. With this client, we traced the origin back to an event that happened during his early childhood.

The event took place in school, which is commonly the case with many shyness and confidence issues. During the first seven years of our life, we are easily impacted by mini or major traumas (emotional events). These events often stay with us affecting our future behaviour. His event took place in a classroom with a very strict female teacher. He had gone to school that day with a lunch box that contained a red drink. While he was in the classroom, the drink had leaked and formed a puddle on the floor, next to his seat. Although frightened of the strict teacher, he had raised his hand to get the teacher's attention to let her know about the situation. However, there were lots of other children with their hands raised, as the teacher had asked a question. She was methodically going around the group of children, pointing to the ones with their hands up and listening to their answers. With a feeling of dread, he had to wait his turn fearing her response. Eventually, she pointed at him. He told her about the accident, and she then dealt with the situation.

Apply EFT to build confidence

Having identified this event, we tapped on it using EFT. We tapped on the feeling of dread until he could no longer feel it. We tapped on the 'waiting' until it no longer bothered him. We tapped on 'the other children looking at him'. We tapped on every element of the memory until it faded, and he no longer experienced any uncomfortable feelings when he thought about it. I then asked him to 'get back inside the kid as if you are there now. Look through his eyes; see what he saw as if you are looking at that now. Turn up the volume, sounds, smells, tastes, images, etc. and check if you can make anything about that event bother you.'

He took a moment as he tried to regain the old feelings, and then he laughed. He suddenly realized why the sound of a woman's heeled shoes on wood had haunted him throughout his life. As a child, he had had to wait as she walked across the wooden floor. He had felt fearful not knowing how she would react. His mind had connected the feeling of fear and dread to the sound of metal heels on a wooden floor. No doubt in his life, he had had moments of feeling fearful whenever he heard that sound unaware of what was causing it. The mystery was solved. We tapped out the sound until his mind could no longer hear it. It just faded from his memory. The whole memory faded. No matter how hard he tried, he could no longer pull it back.

We then came back to the current time and checked whether or not the client could still access the fear that he had so easily connected to earlier in this session. To his surprise, he could not.

These kinds of issues are not always connected to specific one-off traumas. They can also be caused by low-level traumas, such as criticism. Criticism does not have to be deliberate, it can be delivered with love, but its impact can be devastating when it comes to confidence. I have countless times readdressed criticism and helped clients disconnect from its impact. When they do disconnect from it, they stop feeling it is a personal attack on them and 'who they are'. They then see it for what it was, maybe their parents trying to help them become successful or their parents' issues, etc. Once they realize that, they feel empowered. EFT is fantastic when it comes to releasing us from the impact of our past.

The case of unpredictable parenting

Another interesting case I worked with involved a young female client who had a job, which involved speaking in front of her male colleagues. These colleagues were much older than her. However, she was highly qualified. Whenever she presented, she found herself feeling like a little kid. She found it difficult to stand confidently in front of her peers and project confidence. She came to me, fearful that if she did not do something about this problem, it would only be a matter of time before she would lose her high-powered job.

Using EFT, we traced this back to her early childhood. Her father had been highly stressed during those years. As a consequence, he had repeatedly become angry, screaming at her and her brother over minor incidences, such as breaking a cup. This had left the client fearful of making mistakes, trying to avoid his wrath. We tapped through several prominent memories related to these 'dad' traumas. Her confidence naturally grew, she no longer felt intimidated by her male peers.

The future of EFT

EFT has come a long way since its conception in the 1990s. Its dramatic rise was supported by technological advancements that made global communication accessible to the masses, the Internet. Gary Craig, the developer of EFT, embraced these new techniques. It enabled him to reach across the world in a way that had not been possible before the development of the Internet. As a man educated in marketing techniques, he employed a strategy to make EFT available to ordinary people. He marketed it as a self-help technique, one which anybody could learn. People were encouraged to learn it so that they could not only use it on their issues but also on those of their family and friends. He made it easy for therapists to train in EFT and encouraged them to teach as many people as possible. The beauty of this strategy was that EFT did not rely on being accepted by the status quo. New ideas are often resisted. We only have to look back through history to see that. There was a time in history when it was thought that the earth was flat. Those who challenged this idea by saying it was round were mocked and ridiculed. Now, if anyone were to suggest the earth was flat, they would be laughed at and thought of as lacking in education. In time, this will happen with EFT sceptics. The results that EFT yields speak for themselves. More and more people are discovering

EFT every day. Its acceptance by mainstream medicine is only a matter of time.

The future

My vision

For me, I see myself expanding my EFT training. I love teaching therapists how to get results using it. I love doing live demonstrations. I also love innovating. With my knowledge of energy therapies, I developed a simple approach called Inner RePatterning. I intend to train more and more people in energy therapies, both EFT and Inner RePatterning.

EFT: For relationships

by Wendy Fry

My journey to EFT

In 2006 on a holiday in Wales, it dawned on me that I felt unfulfilled and unhappy about my life and what I had achieved. I felt that I had a lot of sadness within me that I did not understand and from that point, my healing quest began.

In my late twenties, I had been diagnosed with depression, suffered anxiety and panic attacks, and had low self-esteem. Knowing how low I could get, I wanted something different for myself. It is as if I simply woke up from the nightmare and realised I had a choice to stay in a pit of despair or begin to take responsibility for making the rest of my life the best of my life.

My journey into holistic health started with Reiki for self-healing. This allowed me the opportunity to let go of some childhood grief around my parents splitting up and believing I was unlovable. Working through and releasing the sadness I experienced enabled me to gain a sense of self-belief and purpose. I then went on to train further to use Reiki with others and, from that point, my whole world opened up. That initial catalyst kindled an inner passion to help others ease their own pain.

In 2008, I set up my own business *Be Positive*, with the aim of helping others to help themselves. I went on to train as a Life and Performance Coach, an NLP practitioner, a hypnotherapist, and an EFT and Matrix Reimprinting practitioner, along with training in many other healing modalities to help others transform their lives into all they could be.

I have since written a book *Find YOU, Find LOVE: Get to the heart of love and relationships using EFT* and have never looked back. It has been through learning these amazing mind-management and energy-psychology techniques that I have been able not only to resolve my own personal pain but to assist others to move beyond theirs too.

Having now built up thousands of client hours and having the privilege of working with so many wonderful people, I feel my life has now 'self-actualised'. I love what I do with a passion and feel so blessed to have experienced these personal shifts and to have aided others to regain a sense of hope and possibility for all that can be achieved with a little self-awareness.

I use EFT every day of my life. It does exactly what it says and provides emotional freedom when things become overwhelming. I share this technique with all who are open to it, as it is so beneficial in creating positive change.

My ongoing quest is to offer others self-management techniques that they can apply independently as and when they need to work through emotions that have become overwhelming. I work with adults and children in person and via Skype and also offer workshops, tailor-made days and programmes of support to aid others to get back on track to creating a life worth living.

Case Study

Challenging Relationship – Jenny

Jenny was born into the world with alcoholic parents. Her mother was in and out of psychiatric care. Life was very chaotic growing up and Jenny spent periods of time in and out of foster care. Life, love and relationships for most of Jenny's young life were traumatic. Years would go by when she never saw her mother. Her father had affairs and introduced her to 'new aunties', none behaving as Jenny's desired mother figure as they were not able to show her the love, time and care that she craved. It was hard for Jenny to trust that love was possible, as she had closed off the idea that she was lovable. Jenny felt incredibly lonely, confused and neglected for much of her early life and it was hard for her to realise that, despite this, she was in fact worthy of being loved by another.

Working with Jenny, using EFT and the Spotlight Process – a unique technique that I have developed to get to the heart of love and relationship problems – we explored where Jenny's fears came from. Nothing was certain for her growing up and she believed that men were unreliable and could not be trusted not to cheat on women and that love was unpredictable. Jenny held the belief and had a fear that 'love would be taken away from her'. This belief was formed in childhood very much based on the fact that her own mother was taken away many times into psychiatric care. She never knew when her mum would return and was not allowed to see her mum in hospital. Her needs as a child were not met adequately enough for her to form positive beliefs about love and relationships in later life and it felt unsafe for Jenny to love, as love from others was unreliable.

Jenny was reluctant to believe that she would find lasting love and was scared of taking risks. She wanted very much to be in a relationship and to have her own children so that she could give to them the love that she felt she never had growing up.

We worked together using EFT to clear the unhappy and traumatic memories from the past. We worked through low self-esteem issues and also transformed the grief and loss of not having the kind of parents that she would have liked. We worked on forgiveness of her parents, so that Jenny could set herself free from the heartache of her past and also acknowledge that it was not her fault that she did not receive the love and care that she needed growing up. Jenny was able to resolve and work through many layers of built-up emotions using the Spotlight Process and EFT. The change in Jenny's confidence, self-worth and self-esteem was amazing. Her feedback to me in an email after our work together was completed was 'I wake up every day now believing in myself.'

Jenny contacted me recently to say that she had got back in touch with a school friend and to tell me that she has been dating him for some time and that they are living together and planning to get married. Jenny's sense of self-love had grown immensely. She said she believed that now she could achieve anything she set her mind to.

Jenny cleared past traumatic events using EFT. She worked through limiting beliefs about her lovability and has learned to love herself first, to look after her own needs, rather than be dependent on another to provide what she can provide for herself. She no longer rejects herself or feels unloved if her fiancé goes away for a weekend or is home late. She trusts fully and completely that she is a wonderful person worth loving, regardless of how others behave or act towards her.

Jenny has come such a long way. She has blossomed into a wonderful young woman. She transformed the emotions she had been carrying with her from the past and now focuses fully on the future and all that is possible for her.

EFT is a transformational tool that moves us beyond our limiting emotions. It is effective for working through past relationship traumas as well as current relationship difficulties.

I use the Spotlight Process and EFT with individuals, families and couples, as well as in my 'Find YOU, Find LOVE' workshops.

The future

As EFT becomes more popular, showing up in the press and on TV, more and more people are turning to a natural support aid to manage everything from PTSD and phobias to anxiety, fears, depression and chronic illness.

EFT has featured in the *Daily Mail*, *Sunday Express*, *The Telegraph* and *The Times*. My own work utilizing EFT has been reviewed and written about in the *Natural Health* magazine and *Soul & Spirit* magazine. These are just a few of the documented cases and research articles now available.

It is my honest belief that the world is waking up to holistic alternatives to improving emotional and physical health and wellbeing and to EFT being natural and a technique that, once learnt, can be applied by the user. It is a very cost-effective and time-practical application that allows the person using it to gain a sense of control over their lives.

In my practice, I now teach EFT to all my clients. If they come for a consultation and are distraught we use tapping to enable them to regain composure and be able to share what they want to talk about with ease. My clients say they feel better, more relaxed, happier and more in control by the time they have left a 90-minute session – sometimes, using EFT for only part of that time. All clients have said that they have noticed a benefit, not only during the appointment, but also a lasting benefit afterwards.

On my last check on Amazon, a total of 4,763 EFT books were available. Many of these books have reached bestseller status, showing the demand for EFT. My own work *EFT for Improving Body Image and Self Esteem* has been featured in *Transform Your Beliefs Transform Your Life: EFT Tapping using Matrix Reimprinting* – just one of the bestsellers offered by Hay House. There is a growing army of EFT practitioners around the globe, enabling others to help themselves by teaching and sharing this wonderful technique.

There is much research now available on the effectiveness of EFT at <http://articles.mercola.com> and also a list of stars, actors and sports professionals using the technique available at <http://theamt.com/celebrities.html>.

EFT is a modern technique for a modern world. It can be used to transform past events as well as future fears. Change is certain in the world we live in, and EFT will help us all to manage those life changes as and when they happen.

Step into your power and create a future you will be proud of, using EFT.

EFT: For bereavement and grief

by Maureen Fearon

My journey to EFT

'Are you mad?', a counsellor asked me when I said I was going to specialize in working with the bereaved. This counsellor would never work with any bereaved person until at least a year had passed after their loss.

Of course, I asked why. I was told that it was because the bereaved are so emotionally out of control and too hard to work with. I will always remember that because it lit a fire in me. Those suffering need help as close to the loss as possible. I hate to see suffering when there is a safe and healthy solution. However, it is widely believed that 'only time is the healer' as well as 'you never get over it'.

It gives me great pleasure to say that those two statements are not true and there is a choice, a solution to this painful emotional roller coaster, which we will probably all experience at some point.

I talk frequently on BBC radio up and down the country and find it interesting which elements of loss are featured. Rarely (unless I am speaking) are people told that there is something they can do, what that is and how to access it. Rather, they will focus on how loss can affect relationships, when is the right time to look for a new partner, how to deal with the processing of the will and how loss can cause heart problems and even lead to death by a broken heart. It is a fascinating area for us all.

Personally, I have experienced many deaths. The most painful of all was the unexpected death of Mum. The shock, pain, uncontrollable emotions and the effect on my health was simply dramatic. I would have paid handsomely for the solutions I now provide as a service to those suffering emotionally around losing loved ones.

Most people dread the death of their loved ones. Rarely do we plan for how we will cope with it. Only a handful of clients over the years, where we have worked on other issues, have said that they plan to have me work with them when 'the time comes'. Just think for a moment. Is that a good idea? To plan to minimize our suffering if we can? Of course it is. However, as we human beings are so complex, it is not as simple as that. So many will choose and accept more pain and suffering than they need to. Crazy, is it not?

For me, one of the positives of working with people suffering loss is that they, through the process, learn a very valuable technique (or two), which they can use as and when they need and on other things as well as their loss. Sometimes, just knowing there is something we can turn to is comforting whether we use it or not. Some will use it to shift the pain of loss. Others are happy for the overwhelming element to be managed. That is their choice.

Many people often say to me, 'But it is okay to be emotional' – I totally agree! They often assume incorrectly that I disagree with the emotions around loss. That is not the case at all. I want people to know about alternatives and to have a choice if they want to suffer less. I would have liked the choice; it could have helped me so much, for example, it could have:

- Given me self-control at the funeral (I cried uncontrollably. I really didn't want to);
- Allowed me to sleep;
- Avoided my nearing anorexia (Feeling constantly sick I stopped eating and lied about eating);
- Most of all, I could have avoided the miscommunication with my lovely husband, which began the path to our splitting up.
- Hindsight is a wonderful thing.

My technique

'So what do you do when you have a bereaved client, Maureen?' Not surprisingly, every session is unique. Some clients can be overwhelmingly emotional; others numb and blocked; some even want to escape as soon as they arrive (they always stay, though). Inner RePatterning and EFT methods are the main tools I use. We focus on what is present and let that guide us to success. Examples of what a client suffering loss may say, when asked what their current challenge is, include:

- 'I can't stop crying'
- 'I feel so lost'

- 'I feel so alone'
- 'Part of me feels dead'
- 'I have this big ache in my chest (head, stomach and other areas of the body)'
- 'I just don't know what I am doing anymore'
- 'I feel so guilty'
- 'I can't get the images out of my head'
- 'I am not sleeping, I can't think straight and I feel like the walking dead'
- 'I feel so desperate'
- 'I am numb and my mind is not working properly'
- 'I feel I am letting people down'
- 'I have no interest in anyone, anything – I don't care anymore'
- 'I don't want to go on. I want the pain to end and don't care if I die now'
- 'I need techniques to cope with the times when I break down, which can be unexpected, and when I have done enough crying'
- 'I feel so angry'
- 'I feel so cheated'
- 'I can't sleep'
- 'I won't eat'
- 'I don't know'. (Yes, they did not know what their issue or current state was.)

All answers give perfectly good places to begin working. Even the 'I don't know' is great to start with and can quickly reveal the emotions which need resolving. It is common to go from a calm, controlled 'I don't know' to overwhelming tears and emotion very quickly. Everyone is different. Those emotions can shift quickly or be huge and stubborn. It takes as long as it needs and I always plan to overrun and make sure the client has plenty of time. In a session, time stands still and 2 or 3 hours can pass in what feels like 20 minutes. The key to my success is that a client leaves **only** when he or she is feeling better and we have tested it. They are happy with that and so am I.

Some in my industry consider me to be a bit of an adventurer. Maybe that is what really led me to setting up a bereavement support group, bringing together people raw in grief to learn coping and emotional-easing techniques. Can you imagine what my counsellor friends said about my doing this? I would not recommend practitioners attempt this without considering all aspects of it seriously, as potentially there is a room of volatile, emotional explosions ready to blow up and, sometimes, they do. It is your responsibility as a practitioner to ensure everyone is safe and that includes emotionally safe. With humans, spilled emotions can trigger us to be emotionally active. Rather like a cascading line of dominoes. When one person falls, they can powerfully nudge others to fall over. All have to be looked after carefully, without neglecting anyone. It is like spinning plates, which will explode if they drop! If a practitioner is easily affected by such deep and powerful pain and sadness in others, I would recommend they choose other types of groups to work with to release those reactions which could lead to problems. However, it is possible to run effective sessions, as the world of NLP (Neuro Linguistic Programming) shows, if one person can do it, we can use their model and achieve the same result.

In the group sessions, there have been tears, laughter, physical pain, despair and the most amazing stories of the mind playing out as emotional healing takes place. For some, working in a group is not for them and, of course, that is okay. Even if they only come to a group session once, they walk away with an understanding of what they can do to help themselves, knowing there are professionals like me they can work with one to one.

People often say to me, 'Surely you find it upsetting working with people in despair.' Many people believe that is inevitable but I am living proof that it is not. That does not make me hard, cold or uncaring. In fact, I care massively. Somewhere, I read that psychologists/ scientists have proven that we are thinking either emotionally or strategically at any one time. Simply, I stay on the strategy side and am able to keep focused on being their guide to feeling better and explaining to them what is appropriate for them to understand at that time. Just like going to the doctor's, you would not expect the doctor to cry when you tell them that you have been afflicted with a health problem. The methods I use can be likened to 'medicine needed to heal emotions'. One small tablet may be enough for some, others need a course of six. Some clients just want what they call the 'Fix' others need to know about how and why the methods work. It is good to plan how you will deal with different clients, identifying which emotions need to be worked on and how to educate clients to help themselves. Maybe we can talk about how that can be easily achieved in Gillian's next book.

The future

Now a question for you. What will you do when you have unwanted loss emotions?

1. Ignore them;
2. Pretend they are not happening;
3. Let them stop you having joy and happiness;
4. Do a bit of DIY work;
5. Take action and book a session with a practitioner?

Truly, what will you choose?

Spread the word so that we can minimise emotional suffering. Let us experience peace and the joys of life as much as we can. You know it makes sense.

EFT: For pets and their people

by Ferris Jay

My journey to EFT

When we love our pets, there is nothing in the world that brings us more joy than having them in our lives. They are our best friends, our faithful companions, our confidants. When they become unwell, suffer in old age or leave us, there is nothing harder for us to bear.

That is where I come in and where I use EFT to help both the pets that I work with and their owners or guardians.

I have worked with pets for over 14 years, initially using energy-healing and communication techniques but, more recently, I have added EFT into the mix. After using it with great results in my personal life, I knew I had to integrate it into my client work.

For my animal work, it felt like EFT was the missing piece in the puzzle. Prior to using it, I had always had good results but I knew there was more that I could do and I wanted to work more closely with the pets' people, as I saw how deeply they needed help for themselves as well as needing help for their pets.

I was right. As pet people, we get incredibly stressed and upset when our animals become unwell. Typically, we push our needs back and focus on helping our furry (or feathered or scaled) friends. We agonise about what might be wrong with them, what treatments to use and how they might be feeling. We can feel horribly helpless and powerless, and suffer immensely as we focus on their condition.

Yet, our pets pick up on our emotions; so when we fret, they feel it. When I started using EFT in my practice, the results were confirmation that it was the tool I had been waiting for. It was perfect for helping people to get relief from the confusion and upset around what is happening to their pets. I found that my clients were able to make better decisions, to cope better with their pets' conditions and as a bonus they learned how to use EFT for their own pets to help them heal.

It was a real win-win situation, as I found the pets healed faster when I worked with their human companions too. When I started integrating surrogate EFT (tapping on myself but for the benefit of the pet) into my distance-healing sessions, the results improved again.

Now, I have what I feel is the magic formula and EFT tapping is that special ingredient that binds all the other elements together.

Case study

Using EFT for pet loss and end of life care

An area of pet work which is dear to my heart and utilizes EFT beautifully is end-of-life work/palliative care. It can bring comfort to the pet and clarity and support to the owner. It helps people monitor their pets' quality of life and assess their options in a balanced way. Often, I find the owners are suffering profoundly from 'anticipatory pet bereavement' and they are mourning the loss of their pet while their pet is still alive and finding it hard to face 'the inevitable' or to know when to let go.

One example of this scenario involved a client who I will call Maureen. Her sweet cat, who we will call Bunny, had 'illness X' and Maureen was devastated, especially after losing her other cat only the year before. She had bonded closely with Bunny, whom she had rescued and rehabilitated.

When I first made contact with her, she was having panic attacks because of the situation. She was temporarily working from home in order to 'be there' for Bunny. The treatment that Bunny was receiving, including having his lung drained of fluid build-up was hard on his system and she knew it was only a temporary measure. She had regular visits from the home vet, who was trying to prepare her for 'the inevitable' but Maureen was desperate to keep Bunny with her for as long as possible because she just could not face losing him.

I worked with both Maureen and Bunny for several weeks. Here is how I used EFT to help them:

I did remote surrogate tapping for Bunny to help his system cope with the treatment and to keep him comfortable. That means that I focused on Bunny's condition and symptoms and did EFT on myself, but for Bunny. For example, if his breathing was laboured, I would tap for that; if he was hiding and shy, I would tap for that. To rate the intensity, I used my intuition. I advise clients just to guess the intensity when working with their own pets.

I did supportive tapping with Maureen, via Skype, to reduce her anxiety and help her come to terms with Bunny's acute condition. Because her anxiety was easily triggered and could result in a panic attack, I had to start by using specific tapping styles, which I combined with supportive energy techniques to help her feel calm enough that she could tune into her emotions without triggering an attack.

I showed Maureen how to use the EFT for herself, so she could gain control when she felt a panic attack coming on. This helped her to trust that she could stay calmer and could deflate the panic when it started to rise within her.

I showed her how to do surrogate tapping for Bunny so she could help him when symptoms presented themselves. I also showed her how to use tapping to help her communicate her feelings to Bunny (see example in 'A happier ending').

Outcome

Through my work, Bunny was looking brighter and seemed more buoyant whilst Maureen was calmer. I felt the sessions helped them re-bond. For example, after sessions, Bunny would come up for cuddles with Maureen as he used to do, whereas before starting the EFT he had begun to hide and had become withdrawn.

The sessions also helped Maureen come to terms with having to make the decision about when to let Bunny go, as he was determined to stay alive, even though his quality of life was deteriorating. The tapping helped her face her emotions and fears in a safe way that did not re-traumatize her.

A happier ending

For me, the most precious part of this end-of-life work is opening the possibility for both pet and person to experience it as a celebration of their relationship and time together, rather than a time of loss.

I did some tapping with Maureen to encourage her to remember their good times and I showed her how to tap to communicate her feelings to Bunny whilst spending time with him, for example, talking to him about how much she adores him and reminding him of their adventures together and how they will always have a heartfelt connection.

As a result, even though it was still hard for her to make the decision, she was able to do it with love and less raw pain than without the tapping and she was able to keep a strong connection with Bunny whilst making that decision. I feel that really helped her cope, even afterwards. There was still a grieving process after Bunny passed away, but she had the tapping to support her through the emotions.

One thing I notice is that often others, partners, co-workers, etc. do not understand the intensity of the grief and pain we feel when we lose a beloved pet; so we can feel isolated in our grief and misunderstood. The tapping is a great way to address these feelings of isolation; of not being understood. Tapping on those issues also helped Maureen to move forward.

The future

The more I work with EFT, the more scope I see for using it to help our pets to better health and to help those who love them to deal with the distress of them being unwell.

EFT is a very empowering technique, a gateway to feeling less helpless in the face of adversity and a simple, yet effective tool to enable us to have an active role in our pets' healing or in their palliative care.

I love my work and being of service to pets and pet people. I already have free resources (currently a free video series showing how to tap for your pets) and paid packages for working with pets and their people worldwide. I am in the process of creating a self-study course for pet owners who want a deeper understanding of how to use EFT simply and effectively for their pets.

I intend to extend my work further to help those who help the animals of our planet, including those involved in animal rescue. I see the horrors they have to witness when they rescue mistreated and abused animals and then the distress of working in systems where they may be responsible for deciding who lives or dies at a rescue centre. I know I will work in some capacity to help those loving people deal with the intense compassion fatigue that many of them suffer from. I also know that EFT will be my tool of choice for that work.

EFT: For emotional eating

by Kathryn Pearson

My journey to EFT

EFT came into my life at an emotionally turbulent time and it totally transformed my emotional state. I went from being the most negative person I knew to someone who noticed the little things, found joy in everything I did, had the confidence to quit my job and become an EFT practitioner. I have had a life–long interest in nutrition, diets, food habits, emotional eating and people's beliefs about food and eating. I have also always wanted to be a 'holistic therapist'. I never knew how I could combine my interests and desire to be some kind of therapist helping people, until I found EFT. It was a natural fit and as soon as I had found my therapy, things evolved quickly and naturally. I never wanted necessarily to help women lose weight; more to help them eat normally, stop obsessing about food and be able to have the same balanced, happy and practical relationship with food I have.

I now use EFT to help women overcome their triggers to emotional eating, such as stress, boredom, loneliness and worry. I also use EFT to change women's relationship with food – including re-writing their limiting beliefs (formed in childhood or by important people in their lives) about how, when and why they should eat. We were not born to reach for the chocolate after a stressful day or to treat ourselves to an indulgent meal when we did something to be proud of – it is all learned behaviour that keeps women, especially, stuck; hating their relationship with food, feeling out of control, hating their weight or body image. I have also found that women use weight as a measure of success and use it to punish themselves, often subconsciously. Keeping themselves overweight because they do not feel good enough for that new relationship, that new job, promotion or success 'I may as well stay this weight because I'm not good enough to be loved', or 'what's the point in applying for that job? I'm not good enough – I'm overweight.'

My ultimate goal is that my clients never diet again; they make peace with food and their body image.

So many women fail to achieve their greatness because they cannot control their eating habits. Because of their body weight, they have low self-esteem, which, in turn, allows the media and other people to make them feel like failures. They do not achieve their potential because they are deemed 'overweight' or 'not in control' or 'not worthy'.

I am here to break this cycle and allow women to break free from their food history and regain their control and freedom.

Case studies

Case study 1

'I had just come to the conclusion that I couldn't and wouldn't change because I didn't know how to.'

When I met Sarah, she was in emotional turmoil. She had moved back from Spain after a painful break up. She had lost her business, cars, money and home. She was slowly starting to rebuild her life back in the UK with a new partner and her daughter, with help from family. Her relationship with her mum was quite 'traumatic' but her main presenting problem was her frustration with herself, especially her 'self–destructive' tendencies to do with her diet and drinking habits and her lack of motivation towards her own business.

She knew what she needed to do but she could not do it. Something was stopping her. She was 'stuck' in a cycle of self-destruction. She wanted to be thinner and lose weight but she kept binge eating and drinking wine. She wanted to build her own beauty business in her local area but she was not promoting herself in any way. She wanted to stop dieting and feeling obsessed about food and exercise, but she did not know how. She wanted to be kind and loving to her partner, but, instead, she took her frustration out on him.

She knew something had to change but she did not know where to start.

Over three sessions, I worked with Sarah to clear these issues. Some were very easy for Sarah to let go of – especially the barrier that was holding her back from starting and promoting her business.

After just one session, Sarah had set up meetings with a business mentor, designed and printed leaflets, posted a huge batch of the leaflets and even booked in real clients! She immediately stopped drinking wine mid-week, which was her hiding mechanism 'I can't face doing any work tonight, I'll have some wine'... 'I can't do any work today. I feel rough from drinking'.

She also easily let go of her frustrations towards herself and realised that she was hurting her partner because of her own lack of motivation and fears. The two almost went hand in hand, which is often found with EFT. Once one problem or issue has been addressed, it leads on to another. In Sarah's case, by addressing her problems, she became more kind and loving and no longer took out her frustrations on her husband – because she had cleared her frustrations!

Bigger stuff for Sarah was her diet history. It had been ingrained in her that diets were a way of life. There was always a new diet or exercise plan to try, with the promise of being better than the last, or giving better results than ever before. If you were not on a diet, then you were just getting fat! Sarah had tried every diet going and, reaching her forties, she realised that diets were obviously not the answer. She, again, knew what she had to do, but just could not do it. She wanted to give up diets. She had reached the point in her life when diets no longer served her. We had to delve into her past and we worked a lot with her beliefs, often called limiting beliefs – stuff we pick up from other people or external circumstances which shape our life. No one was born with the belief that they are fat and so had to be on a diet. She also described how she grew up in a generation of dieters, all her friends were on diets and so she needed to be too. Diets were a way of life.

Sarah had spent so much of her life dieting that she did not trust herself to eat normally, even though she had a vast amount of knowledge about 'healthy' food. She ultimately believed she would get fat if she was not on a diet, so we worked to clear that along with other issues around her beliefs about weighing herself, portion size, body image and using food as a reward.

Sarah had a complete turnaround; although it took a few weeks, she did stop dieting! She quit! She regained her confidence and control and, although Sarah has not reported any drastic weight loss, she shifted about half a stone by controlling her drinking. She now eats much more healthily but, subconsciously, she chooses to eat healthily rather than restricting her food intake. She no longer feels guilty when she has a treat and can enjoy alcohol in moderation. She did briefly go into panic mode when she booked her yearly holiday but with, my gentle reminders about EFT, she was able to do the tapping for herself and did not slip back into old habits of starving herself for a month so she could eat what she wanted on holiday! What I find amazing about Sarah is that she is in control and balanced. She does not worry about what she eats. She sees her food intake as fuel for her body.

When I met her, she was frantic. Her energy was nervous and buzzing. Now, when I see her, she is calm, in control and happy. It makes me so thankful I have this amazing tool to share!

Case study 2

When I met Katie, she was 'desperate'. Her children had left home and gone off to university (one of her children had actually moved abroad and was living a 'dream life'). Her husband worked away but had health problems and she lived in constant fear that his health would deteriorate. Her relationship with her mum was very strained to say the least. They hardly spoke, never saw each other and Katie had constant feelings of resentment towards her mum. All of which were affecting her eating habits, big style. She was comfort eating on a tremendous scale and Katie was worried she was gaining weight quickly and she would end up 'lonely, fat and alone' (her words, not mine!).

Katie was a model client. She entered into her EFT sessions completely open minded and honest. She held nothing back and fully surrendered her trust to me and the EFT process. I believe this was the key for Katie's transformation. We had three sessions where we worked on her worries, fears, loneliness and unhappiness. Katie felt the energy shift in all these areas. During sessions, she was amazed at the feelings EFT gave her. She could literally feel the blockages clearing and experienced the fizzy, light flowing feeling you get when your body is in perfect harmony and the energy is circulating correctly. The real nitty-gritty came when we tapped on her mum and her relationship and past experiences. Some sessions were a little more upsetting than others but Katie always left feeling happier.

Within a week, Katie noticed her snacking had diminished and after a few weeks, she actually texted me concerned that she had lost her appetite! She was, in fact, still eating her three meals a day, but nothing else. This was so alien to Katie she thought something was wrong! She was so used to comfort eating that, when it stopped, she started to worry. It did not take me long to persuade her that this was a good thing. Three months on, she reported a loss of 16lbs. Her eating habits had totally changed and she was a very happy customer. More importantly to me and her, her relationship with her mum had been transformed. Before, she could barely speak to her mum, now she was actually inviting her mum for lengthy stays in her home! It was a beautiful thing to be able to facilitate and Katie was so happy that she had been able to change her relationship with her mum.

Katie still to this day describes her time with me as if a switch had been turned on and she sees things very differently now. Emotional eating is such a common problem for many women. There seems to be a cycle of unhappiness or negative emotion (stress, anxiety, worry, boredom, loneliness), which results in women reaching for food or drink. This binge or snacking leads to feelings of guilt, regret, hopelessness, frustration and fuels any fire you have where you think 'I'm not good enough', and 'I will never succeed'. It can also result in weight gain – another pain point for women.

It is so important to realize that emotions play such a huge role in how we act. The more aware of our emotions we can become, the more awareness we can create. When we are aware of our problems, they become less of a problem! They become less of a struggle and more manageable. I am so happy to have helped these and many more women who have been stuck in a cycle of self–punishment and who have let food rule their lives.

The future

I love helping women with these issues and I love the power of EFT. I have just released a 90-day personalized programme, addressing the most common areas of dieting and food issues women face. I hope to run this, successfully helping women regain their confidence and control when it comes to food. However, I know there is more work to be done. I just wish I had learned about EFT, energy, Law of Attraction and much more when I was younger – my life would have been so different! As I have experience of working with teenagers, I see their struggles and fears. I want to use EFT and my awareness and knowledge to help younger women move through fear, pain and limiting beliefs. I want to evolve my work to help these younger women too. I hope to develop a way of doing this in the very near future!

EFT: And children

by Brad Yates

My journey to EFT

I like to think of my work as similar to how Michelangelo viewed sculpting: the masterpiece is already inside each person … it is just my job to help clear away what does not belong. I am grateful for the opportunity to be able to reach so many folks around the world via YouTube but what I really love doing is actually working with people – either individually or in groups – on the phone or live and in person.

I actually started out as an actor but in looking for a backup career to support my family, I trained to become a hypnotherapist. As time went on, I found personal development work to be my real calling. That became even clearer when I was introduced to Tapping. At first, I did a little of it during my hypnotherapy sessions but over time, it became my primary modality for working with folks. I then started experimenting with making tapping rounds available online – first as audios, and then eventually as videos. This opened me up to a global audience, and I enjoy working with clients around the world by phone or Skype, as well as travelling to other countries to do workshops.

Although a lot of folks know me as the author of a best–selling children's book about EFT – *The Wizard's Wish* –, few of my clients have been children.

However, I have been very pleased with what I have seen with kids benefitting from EFT, both in my own work and in the work of others.

The first kids I worked with, naturally, were my own. A favourite experience was tapping on my daughter as a toddler when she had hiccups. I just gently held her and tapped under her arm, and the hiccups quickly ended. My son has also found tapping to be very beneficial in preparing for tests, helping him to calm down and be more focused.

Case studies

'Lydia'

Two of my favourite experiences of tapping with children occurred with the kids of friends. The first was a 10-year -old girl who I will call Lydia. She had experienced an increasing amount of anxiety, to the point where she was no longer able to attend school. A mutual friend had shared a copy of *The Wizard's Wish*, and the night Lydia and her parents read it and did some tapping was the first night in a long time that Lydia had been able to fall asleep easily. Her mother asked if I could work with her and we did some tapping together, exploring what she was feeling, and what might be the cause of her anxiety. As she became calmer, I suggested we take a drive over to school, which we did. Once there, she was able to get out of the car, but did not yet feel ready to go in. Her mum and I acknowledged her courage in coming this far and encouraged her to see it as a victory.

While we did not work together again, I heard that, not long afterwards, she did start attending school again. She had a special arrangement with the school that, when she felt herself becoming uncomfortable, she could leave the room to find a private place to tap and clam herself down again.

The next time I saw her was several months later at a track event, where she was participating fully, with no visible discomfort. This was particularly encouraging given the fact that it was crowded … not to mention that athletic competitions often add a certain amount of stress. Lydia had come a long way thanks to tapping.

'Ben'

Another friend asked me to work with her son, whom I will call Ben. He was eight at the time and up until then, had loved playing baseball. Getting hit by the pitcher changed that, though, and he found himself unable to go up to bat. We talked and tapped for a bit, acknowledging the pain he felt from the blow and exploring his fears. The calming effect of the tapping allowed him to voice his fears, including the fear that he would die if he got hit by a pitcher again. As he said it, while tapping, he recognized that it was highly unlikely and not a fear that he needed to hold on to. By the time we were done, he reported that he not only felt calm about playing again but was also excited to get back to his favourite pastime. His mum told me shortly afterwards that he was back to playing baseball with his former joy and gusto.

The future

As more and more people experience these kinds of results, I can only imagine that EFT will spread. The initial resistance is understandable – not only does it look a bit strange to most people but there is also a tendency to resist anything that might actually create change. Acknowledging that, persistence by those who share this and an underlying tendency for humans to evolve in spite of themselves will allow this process to grow in popularity. I look forward to continuing to share EFT via YouTube, as well as visiting more places around the world to tap with folks live and in person – such a wonderful and energetic experience!

Acknowledgements

I am extremely grateful for the enormous amount of support I have received in the long process of writing this book. Specifically, from my husband Paul, who has shown unwavering support and patience with me; my children, other family members and friends and especially my mum being my most ardent supporter on this journey in countless ways. Thanks Mum xx

Thank you to my daughter Rebecca for her support, advice, insights, proofreading and encouragement.

I would never have even dreamed about writing a book without the guidance and help from a friend and therapist, Jane Reid.

The North West EFT UK group, my friends at The Harmony Hub and my work colleagues have also been a valuable support both in practical matters and in confidence building.

Particular thanks go to Mark Bristow who has mentored me throughout this whole process, having been further down the road on his own book-writing journey. His support, advice and guidance has been invaluable and without it, this book would not be here!

A humongous thanks to all the wonderful co-authors who work with EFT and who have kindly shared their stories and insights with us so we can all learn from them; especially for their patience and support throughout this process.

Heartfelt thankyou to Jack Canfield for his support and encouragement as evidenced in the wonderful foreword he so graciously wrote.

Thank you so much to the lovely people who have taken time to read and review the book: Mary Ayers, Pamela Bruner, Karl Dawson, Mary Hernon, Helen Humphries & Fabrizio Poli

Thank you Manoj Vijayan for your never ending patience and the amazing graphics on the book cover design.

Deborah Hartmann and Hannah Briggs. I cannot say thank you enough for all your patience with my many questions especially with my inexperience in the process and the to-ing and fro-ing with the many co-authors chapters.

Thank you to Dawn & Phil Owen for the graphics, website, technical and business support.

I am very honoured and blessed to have gone on this journey and for all the people who have supported me.

A heartfelt thank you to each and every one of you.

About the author

Gillian Morris is an Advanced Emotional Freedom Techniques Practitioner, a Reflexologist and Reiki Practitioner. Gillian lives in Lancashire, England with her husband, Paul. They have three grown up children. She has a deep love of nature, animals and learning which has led her to where she is today.

Gillian has worked in the education system, with young people and adults with learning difficulties and disabilities, for over fifteen years and she uses the skills, knowledge and expertise learned there with clients in her private practice.

She has suffered chronic health conditions, which affected her everyday life for over 30 years, she is grateful to be healthier and much more active due to learning and using EFT.

Today, she has her own business, working with clients of all ages on a variety of issues. Her passion is to get EFT out into the main stream to inform and empower people to live happier, healthier lives. She does volunteer work with a local church group and is an active member of the NW EFT UK Group.

Gillian's website is www.gillianmorriscoaching.com

EFT Co-authors' details

Tania Aranda

Tania is a professional who is passionate about working and succeeding in International business environments. Mother of two wonderful boys who need lots of energy and patience to guide, care and love, hoping her efforts result in confident, loving, brave men who are prepared to face the world. Wife of a loving and kind man, to whom she hopes to be the best partner in life, a friend who is there to listen laugh, cry, hold your hand or encourage when needed. She is a woman seeking for continuous personal and spiritual growth, desiring to be connected to pure feminine power. She is also a passionate EFT practitioner who understands and connects with women's issues and challenges of today.

She supports her clients, who struggle finding balance between the demands and expectations women face on daily basis. She holds her clients in a safe, loving space where they can easily release the negative emotions and work with them to knock down the limiting beliefs which hold them back, so they can unleash their full feminine power, and live gracefully, lovingly and full of joy.

Her purpose is to reach as many women as possible, who are ready to discover their inner voice and reveal the Goddess who lives inside of them; to connect with their inner child and be playful; to connect with their creativity, deepest wishes and desires; to feel passion, sexy and sensual, and just like the caterpillar transforming into a beautiful colorful butterfly, how a woman is meant to be.

Contact:
Mobile: +32 (0)4788 49211
Website: http://www.taniaaranda.com/
Email: tania.arandaeft@gmail.com

Emma Bailey

Emma is a qualified EFT, Inner Re-Patterning and Reiki Master Teacher/Trainer as well as being a master practitioner of NLP, Hypnotherapy, Time Line Therapy™ and Scenar Therapy.

Emma combines the science and knowledge of EFT, mindfulness and various types of energy medicine with her knowledge of classical horsemanship in order to facilitate emotional, behavioural and physical change in both people and horses.

She is passionate about helping people to develop and nurture their equine partnership, releasing stress and tension, in both themselves and their horses, through learning to 'connect and reflect'. One of her favourite offerings is teaching people to meditate with their horse for physical, emotional and mental transformation.

She offers one-to-one sessions regularly throughout the North West of England both with and without horses, depending on the individual requirements and via skype on an international basis. Emma also runs a wide variety of workshops, clinics and trainings, which are available throughout Europe on request.

Her sessions and workshops are lively and varied as well as peaceful and respectful of both the individual's and group's needs in the moment. She works with all sorts of issues including leadership development, confidence building, releasing trauma, personal development, both physical and mental performance coaching, as well as chronic and complex health issues in horses and humans.

Emma has been a prolific public speaker and event organiser throughout her career and is available for both small groups and international conferences interested in her energy work with horses. Her talks are full of stories, experiential learning and her passion and love for helping horses and people shines through.

Contact:
Website: www.fromhorsestohumans.com
Email : info@fromhorsestohumans.com
Find "From Horses To Humans" on Facebook, twitter and Instagram
Mobile: 07860 564076

Elizabeth Boath

Dr Elizabeth Boath is Associate Professor in Health, academic psychologist and National Teaching Fellow. She is Co-Chair of the AAMET (Association for the Advancement of Meridian Energy Therapies) Research Committee. As an advanced EFT and Matrix Re-imprinting practitioner and trainer, Elizabeth is also a Clinical hypnotherapist, ILM Coach, Emotion Code and Reiki practitioner. She has over two decades' experience of health service research and has published widely in the field of energy psychology. Elizabeth is currently leading UK research into EFT and, inspired by her experience in helping colleagues, students, family and friends using EFT, is seeking research funding to explore its use further. Elizabeth also has particular expertise in clinical effectiveness and research methodology and is a published author with a range of academic books and publications in these areas.

Contact:
Mobile: 07507340147
Email: eftmatrix1@gmail.com

Sharon Branagh

Sharon is a Behaviour Specialist and Therapist with over 25 years' experience working with mental and physical health difficulties. She has a successful private practice in Gloucestershire and is known for giving talks and workshops, which share the vast range of techniques that she uses, including meditation, laughter yoga, EFT and other stress reduction strategies. Sharon teaches the Expert Patients Programme within the NHS, which is a self-management course for people with long-term health conditions. She is also involved in an outreach project working with the population within HM Prison Services.

Sharon is married with two young girls. She is a volunteer for a national charity's telephone support line and runs a local support group. Sharon was diagnosed with a health condition so is an ideal advocate to coach others on their return journey to wellbeing.

Contact:
Website: www.sharonbranagh.co.uk
Email: Sharon.branagh@hotmail.com
Skype: sharonbranagh1
Mobile: 07834855560

Mark Bristow

After over 25 years of working in Financial Services, Mark was living a life of total frustration. He decided to train in NLP (Neuro Linguistic Programming) with the aim of being successful in his day job. He soon realized, however, he was not living his true purpose. In that moment, he decided to quit financial services and to do what he loved, which was to help people change their lives.

Mark loved NLP so much that he trained to Master Practitioner level, and after meeting with EFT (Emotional Freedom Techniques) Master, and creator of Matrix Re-imprinting, Karl Dawson, he also trained in these disciplines, which he described as "the final piece of the Jigsaw".

Mark is the author of the Amazon Best Selling Book *The Financial Healer* and presents *The Spirit of EFT* show on EFT radio.

Mark's life purpose is 'to inspire fresh insights and share wisdom with the world, which if people knew, understood, and acted upon would transform their experience of living'.

Contact:
Website: www.markbristowcoaching.com

Maureen Fearon

Maureen Fearon: NLP Master Practitioner, EFT Trainer, Inner Re-Patterning Trainer, Emotional Specialist, Bereavement Expert, Corporate Trainer, Stress Consultant, MBTI Personality Profiler.

She is internationally renowned as a mentor, a coach, a relationship fixer, a broadcaster, a "one off" comedian, a motivational speaker and is known for her work as a Love Guru! She is simply an expert in human behaviour and emotions, continually motivated by the positive transformations of her clients.

It began with investing in NLP training. 'I was told I needed the certificate to be a coach. Expecting it to be boring and tedious, I couldn't wait for it to start and then be over! Instead, it was life changing. I learnt about the real me, the changes I could make to have dreams come true. Sounds dramatic but that's how it was. Then EFT training provided me with a powerful tool'.

As an emotional specialist, she was the first in the world to be a certified trainer in the dynamic "Inner Re-Patterning" process which she uses with individuals especially with sensitive issues such as loss, abuse and trauma. Maureen trains people to be emotional specialists too. She is noted for her enthusiasm and making complex psychology simple and easy to understand.

Maureen regularly shares her expertise with BBC radio audiences nationally and on the World Service, covering a variety of topics from loss, dating and confidence to workplace challenges, mental health and relationship issues. As an entertaining conference speaker, she leaves audiences with positive lasting impressions and profound messages, which, for many, are life changing.

She also works with disaffected teenagers, helping them to overcome emotional issues and achieve exam success where failure is expected. Teaching them how to begin designing their futures, no matter how their lives started, is a real passion. Her message is to 'overcome suffering and learn to enjoy life'.

Contact:
Website: www.maureenfearon.co.uk

Wendy Fry

Wendy Fry, Emotional Health, Love and Relationship Consultant and author is passionate about helping women to get to the heart of their love and relationship problems.

Qualified as Hypnotherapist, Life and Performance Coach and Practitioner in Advanced EFT, Matrix Re-imprinting, Positive EFT, NLP, Picture Tapping Technique, EMO Flow, Reiki, Matrix Birth Re-imprinting and Future Life Progression, Wendy understands the impact of how our limiting beliefs about our self-worth and lovability influence all relationships and, ultimately, shape our lives.

Author of *Find You, Find Love: Get to the heart of love and relationships using EFT*, a tapping book dedicated to empowering women to believe in themselves despite past circumstances. *Find You, Find Love* includes *The Spotlight Process*, a unique technique Wendy has developed to help you to get to the heart of love.

As a co-author in the Dial a Guru Series of self-help books, Wendy reaches out sharing the tools and techniques to get you back on track to living your life with passion and purpose.

She works with individuals from her private practice in Surrey, UK and internationally over Skype and offers a range of workshops worldwide.

For more information about the full range of services offered, to read her blog or sign up for a free chapter '*Love and Relationship Beliefs*' from her first book *Find You, Find Love* and additional free resources and audio downloads please visit her website.

Contact:
Website: www.wendyfry.com

Ferris Jay

Ferris Jay is an Energy Therapist, EFT practitioner and coach who has been working in the holistic health field for 16 years. She is a passionate up-lifter, helping both people and pets worldwide to thrive and to overcome adversity.

Ferris helps pets to overcome illness, injury, pain and discomfort using natural, non-invasive techniques that complement veterinary care.

She helps pets to improve their quality of life, vitality and happiness.

She empowers their people to be active participants in their pets' healing process and shows them how to avoid the stress, upset and confusion that can arise when care giving for their pet.

Ferris specializes in helping pets to navigate old age with grace and ease and helping their people to come to terms with their pets' mortality.

She helps them enjoy every moment together and cherish their precious memories.

She also offers pet bereavement support for those struggling to cope with the death of a pet, helping them come to terms with their loss, heal their hearts and move forward whilst honoring their pets' memories. Ferris lives in rural Ireland with her furry and feathered friends, and when not having fun working with clients, she can often be found gardening, out in nature or crocheting.

For more information about her pet healing, pet parent coaching and pet bereavement support services, please visit her website where you can download her free video series showing you how to use EFT tapping to help your pet to heal.

Contact:
Website: www.ferrisjay.com

Ferris also helps non pet owners to thrive and you can find out about her personal development coaching, which combines EFT tapping, energy and mindset techniques, at www.thethoughtgardener.com

Lisa Kent

Lisa is an AAMET Certified EFT Practitioner and Business Coach. It is her mission to help solo entrepreneurs and holistic therapists overcome the second-guessing and feelings of unworthiness, which can freeze us in our tracks when it comes to our business.

Lisa uses a combination of marketing knowledge and EFT to create a sturdy, confident foundation for her clients, where thoughts of "am I good enough?" become a thing of the past.

Lisa mostly works one on one via Skype, gently encouraging everyone she works with to feel a deep connection to their inner wisdom, tapping away the usual "small self" concerns and inner chatter. This facilitates a relief from feeling stuck, overwhelmed and worrying about the future, allowing those she works with to recognise their inner strength, gifts and abilities with confidence. Lisa specialises in creating clarity around specific business goals and assisting her clients to experience ease and joyful forward momentum.

Through Lisa's work as a business coach she has mentored many EFT and Holistic Practitioners as they navigate the marketing minefield, and provided a platform for them to learn new techniques and concepts through one on one coaching, short courses and in 'The EFT Marketing Lounge', which is a fun and supportive group on Facebook. https://www.facebook.com/groups/theeftmarketinglounge

Lisa is passionate about helping others succeed in their business, as she understands the emotional stumbling blocks, which can trip up even the most knowledgeable and resilient business owner. Lisa firmly believes that everyone should have the best chance possible of achieving what he or she sets out to do.

Contact:
Website: www.lisakent.com
Email: info@lisakent.com

Deborah Miller

Deborah D. Miller, Ph.D. in Cell and Molecular Biology, EFT Expert and Trainer, Deeksha Giver, Reiki Master, Nutritional Guide, Personal Motivation Guide and Internationally recognised author, is passionate about helping people feel empowered and capable of maintaining a healthy state of mind and body.

Deborah understands the necessity of working with the emotional aspects underlying 'dis-ease' within the body and the need to cleanse and nourish the physical body. Her volunteer work with children with cancer has led Deborah to a heart-felt, passionate and inspired goal of helping a 1,000,000 people prevent future illness, (mental, emotional or physical) using the simplest, easiest and most economical methods.

She is the author of the *The Dragon with Flames of Love*, a Tapping book dedicated to empowering adults and children facing the challenge of a serious illness and *Green Drink Red Drink*, which provides information and recipes on how to add healthy greens to your meals.

Contact:
Websites: www.oaxacaproject.com and www.findthelightwithin.com

Kathryn Pearson

Kathryn Pearson is a former secondary school teacher with over 7 years of experience of working closely with young people. Following a life changing experience, she left her profession to pursue her dreams of helping young people – just like her younger self – who are lonely, bewildered and scared. Now an EFT practitioner and specialised Teen Yoga teacher, she specialises in helping sensitive teens and young women combat stress, fear and worry. Her mission is to give the next generation the confidence and tools to break free from negative thinking and to be able to follow their dreams much earlier than she did! Kathryn is currently writing her first self-help book for teenagers.

Contact:
Website: www.kathrynpearson.co.uk
Or sign up here (http://bit.ly/1JHyPnA) to receive her free de-stress meditation for young people.

Gill Pinnington

Having worked in the private and public sector in a number of high pressure roles, and personally experiencing the resulting and truly debilitating effects of stress, anxiety and depression on personal and professional success, it is Gill's mission to support and empower businesses and teams of all sizes to put health and wellbeing at the top of their agenda so that they can flourish.

Using an integrative approach, with individuals and teams, she utilises EFT, Matrix Re-imprinting, NLP, Hypnotherapy and Fusion Therapeutic Coaching to bring about significant and long lasting change.

She offers workplace wellbeing training and resilience coaching throughout the UK and Europe and individual sessions in Eastbourne or over Skype.

For more information about the full range of services offered, to read Gill's blog or to sign up for a free copy of her e-book '9 Steps to Ultimate Confidence' please visit her website.

Contact:
Mobile: 0753 006 4573
Email: gill@flourishnow.co.uk
Website: www.flourishnow.co.uk

Tania A. Prince

Tania A. Prince, EFT Founding Master, AAMET Accredited EFT Master Trainer of Trainers. ABNLP recognised NLP and Hypnotherapy Trainer.

Tania is an author and conference speaker. She presented at many of the EFT Masterclass Conferences as well as organising the Manchester conference. She has worked in the field of therapy for over twenty-three years. During that time, she has worked with thousands of clients. She has also worked in the Philippines as an EFT therapist and trainer, helping the survivors of the typhoon. In her private practice, she specialises in helping people build their confidence, in performance and public speaking.

Tania is a leading International EFT Trainer. Most of her training courses are run in Central Manchester, England. She has trained therapists and self-help enthusiasts in EFT for sixteen years, both in the UK and internationally. Her trainings are renowned for their humour and depth.

Tania is also the developer of the powerful, mindfulness tapping technique, Inner Re-Patterning. As well as EFT training courses, she runs Inner Re-Patterning and Public Speaking courses.

Contact:
Websites: www.eft-courses.co.uk and www.TaniaAPrince.com

John Soriano

John Soriano, Masters Degree in Education and a Bachelor degree in Psychology. He is an EFT Expert, NLP Master Practitioner, and is an internationally recognised coach. He is passionate about helping people feel empowered about learning and personal performance. John uses his cutting edge achievement techniques with learners of all ages and of all subjects, and helps to overcome test anxiety.

He deals with the inner processes of HOW to learn, and uses EFT to help eliminate emotional blocks to performance and to help transform motivation as well as anger and stress issues. He works one on one with clients all over the world and has appeared on numerous radio shows in the US and the UK. He also works with groups.

Contact:
Website: www.easeoflearning.com

Pete Weaver

Pete Weaver, MSc, CMCIPD, Advanced EFT and Matrix Re-imprinting practitioner, NLP practitioner, Advanced Spiral Dynamics facilitator, Psych-K advanced facilitator, Hypnotherapist, Executive coach, Life coach, LTA registered professional tennis coach and internationally recognized speaker in four continents, is passionate about helping people to fulfil their potential and be the best they can be.

Pete works in the corporate world as an Executive Coach and Management Consultant, using a blend of Energy therapies and other tools. He also works with a leading sports psychologist to help achieve peak performance in athletes and other performers.

He still loves the challenges of both business and sport. He keeps his hand in with interim management projects and still plays County standard tennis.

Contact:
Website: www.hyper4mers.co.uk
Email: paw@globalnet.co.uk

Dulcie Williams

Dulcie Williams – Cert Ed, qualified as a Teacher in UK before becoming a Business, HR, Management & Training Consultant. She subsequently ran her own corporate communications business, travelling all over the UK and London for 12 years. She continues to offer Consultancy in the Care Sector, where she incorporates EFT to great effect for both care givers and clients.

Dulcie uses EFT via skype to help people heal the shock and emotional effects of Cancer diagnosis, treatment, recovery and their 'new normal'. Having 'done Cancer' herself in 2015, Dulcie feels uniquely placed to help. She is positive and supportive - yet never tells anyone 'to be positive or strong'.

Contact:
Email: dulciewilliams@hotmail.com

Brad Yates

Brad Yates is known internationally for his creative and, often, humorous use of Emotional Freedom Techniques (EFT). Brad is the author of the best-selling children's book The Wizard's Wish, the co-author of the best-seller Freedom at Your Fingertips, and a featured expert in the film The Tapping Solution. He has also been a presenter at a number of events, including Jack Canfield's *Breakthrough to Success*. He has done teleseminars with *The Secret* stars Bob Doyle and Dr. Joe Vitale, and has been heard internationally on a number of internet radio talk shows.

Brad also has well over 600 videos on YouTube, which have been viewed over 12 million times, and is a contributing expert on the Huffington Post.

Contact:
Website: www.tapwithbrad.com

EFT: Further reading

Book Title	Author
Financial Healer	Mark Bristow
EFT & Beyond	Pamela Bruner & John Bullough
Tapping into Ultimate Success	Jack Canfield & Pamela Bruner
Try it on Everything	Dr Patricia Carrington
Clinical EFT Handbook Vol 1	Dawson Church & Stephanie Marohn
The EFT Manual	Gary Craig
Matrix Reimprinting using EFT	Karl Dawson & Sasha Allenby
Transform Your Beliefs, Transform Your Life	Karl Dawson & Kate Marillat
Find You, Find Love	Wendy Fry
Mothers and Daughters	Wendy Fry
Heal Your Birth Heal Your Life	Sharon King
The Dragon with Flames of Love	Deborah Miller
The Tapping Solution for Weight Loss and Body Confidence	Jessica Ortner
The Tapping Solution	Nick Ortner
The Tapping Solution for Pain Relief	Nick Ortner
The Wizard's Wish	Brad Yates
Freedom at your Finger Tips	Brad Yates (Co-Author)

EFT: Further resources

Website	Author
http://www.theeftcentre.com/	Sue Beer / Emma Roberts
http://financialhealer.co.uk/	Mark Bristow
http://makeyoursuccessreal.com/	Pamela Bruner
http://www.eftuniverse.com/	Dawson Church
http://www.emofree.com/	Gary Craig
http://www.efttrainingcourses.net/	Karl Dawson
http://www.magicalnewbeginnings.com/	Sharon King
http://taniaaprince.com/	Tania A. Prince
http://www.thetappingsolution.com/	The Tapping Solution
http://traumabustertechnique.com/	Rehana Webster
http://www.eftdownunder.com/energy-techniques/	Steve Wells/David Lake
http://www.bradyates.net/	Brad Yates

References

Dawson, K. & Allenby, S. (2010) Matrix Reimprinting using EFT. London: Hay House.

Meet The Boss. (2016). Retrieved August 25, 2016, from https://meettheboss.tv/.

Seymour, L. & Grove, B. (2005) Workplace interventions for people with common mental health problems, London: British Occupational Health Research Foundation.

The EFT Centre. (2014-15). Retrieved August 25, 2016, from http://www.theeftcentre.com/.

The Tapping Solution Foundation. (2015). Retrieved August 25, 2016, from http://tappingsolutionfoundation.org/ProjectLight.

22091781R00115

Printed in Great Britain
by Amazon